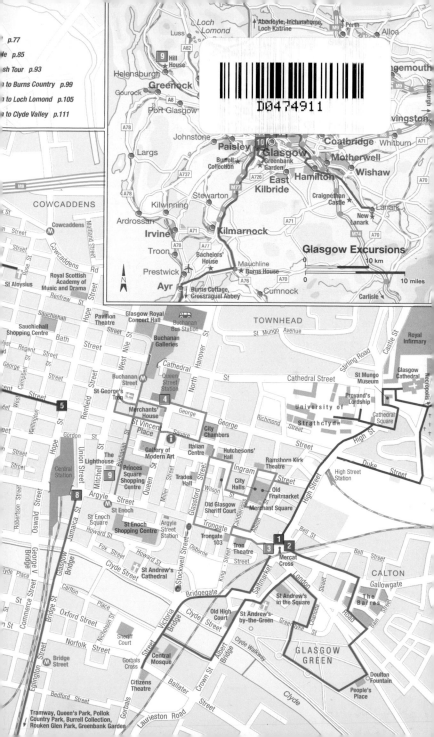

INSIGHT GUIDES

Great Breaks
GLASGOW

Contents

Glasgow's Top 10

From Glasgow's dazzling variety of art and architecture to the wild natural beauty of the surrounding countryside, here, at a glance, are the top sights and activities of this fascinating Scottish city

▲ **Kelvingrove Art Gallery and Museum** *(p.72)*. Discover the wonders of Victorian civic endeavour at this red-sandstone museum filled with compelling exhibits.

▲ **Shopping**. Choose from swanky designers at Princes Square *(p.56)* or quirky boutiques in the Merchant City *(p.45)* and West End *(pp.69 & 81)*.

▲ **Loch Lomond and the Trossachs** *(p.108)*. It's adventures galore in this national park, dipping into Britain's largest lake, trekking and visiting beguiling villages.

▶ **Glasgow culture and nightlife** *(p.10)*. With its myriad music scenes, cutting-edge theatre and nightspots, Glasgow caters for everyone.

Cathedral and Necropolis (pp.20 & 22). Glasgow's impressive cathedral was founded in 1136, while the Necropolis provides spine-tingling moments amid crumbling temples and monuments.

Museum of Transport (p.74). This ever-popular collection of buses, trams, trains, bikes and cars is moving to the striking Riverside Museum in 2011.

Burns Country (p.98). On the trail of the bard, visiting Alloway Kirk's graveyard, Burns Cottage, and the new Robert Burns Birthplace Museum.

Pollok Estate (p.87). A splendid mansion, riverside walks, biking trails, and the world-class Burrell Collection make for a memorable Southside day.

New Lanark (p.113). David Dale and his son-in-law Robert Owen's model factory town is now a fascinating Unesco World Heritage Site.

Glasgow arts scene (p.66). The Glasgow School of Art and assorted galleries give the city one of the world's most vibrant contemporary art scenes.

Overview

The Art of Reinvention

Glasgow is a city continually in flux: its vibrant culture, and its grand architectural splendours of sandstone and steel make it sparkle despite dark urban realities

Glasgow is something of a Renaissance city. Like a proud fighter who refuses to be knocked down, this vibrant, bustling, rumbustious Scottish city is once again busy reinventing itself. Born as a fishing village on the slopes

above the meandering River Clyde, Glasgow has been, in turn, a market town, an ecclesiastical centre, a seat of learning, a city of merchant adventurers, a gateway to the New World, an industrial powerhouse of the British Empire and a European cultural capital.

ARCHITECTURE

Approaching from the south, first impressions are not great. However, despite some misguided 1960s urban planning – Brutalist tower blocks and the M8 motorway which rips through the heart of the city – Glasgow is an architectural treasure house. Its mix of Victorian, Georgian, Venetian and Art Deco equals anything in Europe.

The city retained its grim face until well into the second half of the 20th

century, when the New Glasgow Society – a loose collection of early eco-warriors – led a rearguard action against the City Corporation's policy of 'If it's old, knock it down'. Victorian tenement homes were stripped and refurbished instead of being demolished, revealing honey-and-red sandstone wonders and striking detail. The defining moment in Glasgow's recent past was its selection in 1990 as European City of Culture.

ECONOMY AND RENEWAL

Today the city is once again reviving its fortunes with the bold regeneration of the inner-city riverbank. In 2011 the Zaha Hadid-designed Riverside Museum will add to the shimmering riverside scene. Meanwhile, the Merchant City's abandoned warehouses continue to be transformed into swanky apartments, businesses and restaurants. New arts centre Trongate 103 is at the centre of a plan to regenerate run-down streets and connect the city with the Clyde.

Glasgow boasts some chic shopping centres, such as Princes Square. High-profile events like the biennial Glasgow International Festival and preparations for the Commonwealth Games in 2014 are reinvigorating the city. Its reputation as a dour, violent slum is finally being shaken off and Glaswegians are generally proud of the transformation.

Above: Glasgow's skyline reveals its rich mix of architectural styles. **Below**: the riverside is packed with striking buildings, such as the Science Centre.

LOCATION

The city lies in the wide strath, or plain, of the River Clyde and is sheltered to the north, east and south by high, open ground; it's possible to be in rolling countryside 20 minutes' drive from the city centre. Glasgow is about 26 miles (40km) from the sea at Greenock, and the Clyde starts to widen into the Firth just below the Erskine Bridge at Old Kilpatrick. North of the city, the Campsie Fells rise to 1,900ft (600m) and are dramatically visible from many areas.

CLIMATE

The Gulf Stream warms the whole of the west coast of Scotland, and Glasgow is a beneficiary of more temperate weather than might be expected from its latitude. Winters are generally mild (between 0°C/32°F and 6°C/43°F) with more rain than snow, though cold snaps of as low as -24°C (-11°F) have been known. Summers, in common with the rest of Britain, appear to be growing warmer, with temperatures of up to 25°C (77°F).

However, the prevailing westerly winds which blow across the Atlantic bring with them their fair share of rain. A day which offers glorious sunshine in the morning can become a depression of drizzle by the early afternoon. Go prepared.

Above: the grand Merchants' House (*see p.58*) in 1874.

HISTORY OF TURMOIL

Glasgow was inhabited as long ago as 4000BC, when hunters pushed north in the wake of the retreating ice. Roman general Agricola found hostile tribes in the area in AD80 and threw up a chain of forts across the narrow waist of Scotland. The retreat of the Romans led to centuries of turmoil between warring tribes of Scots, Picts, Britons and Angles.

St Ninian began missionary work in Strathclyde in the 4th century, but St Mungo is credited as the founder of the city in AD543, although only legend bears witness to his arrival. Glasgow Cathedral was founded in 1136 on the site of St Mungo's Church on the banks of the Molendinar, a pretty *burn* (stream). But, although the city was recognised as a respectable seat of learning (Glasgow University was created in 1451) with strong religious traditions throughout the Middle Ages, all the political and military action took place in Edinburgh, Falkirk and Stirling.

INDUSTRIAL AWAKENING

The British Empire spawned Glasgow's development as an important port city. John Golborne's ingenious plan of the

Above: the doomed ocean liner RMS *Lusitania*, pictured here in 1907, was built in the Glasgow shipyards.

The People

Glaswegians have a way with words, even if visitors have difficulty understanding them. The patter, sociologists argue, is a mix of native sharpness, Highland feyness, Jewish morbidity and the Irish *craic* (witty story-telling). Much of Glasgow's story has been harsh, and, in the past, raising a laugh served as an antidote to adversity. The shipyards of the 1960s, for example, have provided plenty of material for Glaswegian-born comedian, Billy Connolly.

Above: Glaswegians are generally very quick and funny.

1770s – to build piers along the banks and allow the river to scour its own bed – turned Glasgow into a serious contender as an Atlantic port.

The 'Tobacco Lords' were the first major merchants; many of their houses still stand. They created not only the tobacco trade with Maryland, Virginia and North Carolina, but a merchant class. Their need for iron tools, glass, pottery and clothes to trade with the colonies was the impetus for the city's awakening to the Industrial Revolution.

Glasgow became a cotton town in 1780. Within a decade, scores of mills were using the fast Scottish rivers to power their looms, and immigrants from Ireland and the Highlands were flooding in. Glasgow's population exploded, from 23,500 in 1755 to a peak of 1,128,000 in 1939. The metal-bashing industries – shipbuilding, ironworks, armaments – were complemented by textiles, chemicals and manufacturing.

During the 20th century, Glasgow shared in the spoils and misfortunes of the industrialised world. There may be no more belching foundries or clanging, but recent city administrations have pragmatically courted private finance to unlock the city's post-industrial potential. New developments and attractions are sprouting everywhere, bringing with them a new sense of civic pride. Glasgow is flourishing once again.

Find our recommended restaurants at the end of each Tour. Below is a price guide to help you make your choice.

Eating Out Price Guide

Two-course meal for one person, including a glass of wine.

£££ over £45
££ £25–45
£ under £25

Guide to Coloured Boxes

E Eating	This guide is dotted
F Fact	with coloured boxes providing additional practical
G Green	and cultural infor-
K Kids	mation to make the most of your visit.
S Shopping	Here is a guide to
V View	the coding system.

Entertainment

PERFORMING ARTS

Glasgow is a thriving centre for the arts, mixing the old with some of Scotland's most cutting-edge scenes. When it comes to the variety of music events, art shows and nightlife, few cities in Britain can compare. For details of performance times and dates, check the local press (*The Herald* and *The List* are the best), or visit www.seeglasgow.com.

Theatre, dance, opera and comedy

The Citizens Theatre (tel: 0141-429 0022; www.citz.co.uk) in Gorbals Street combines iconoclastic drama with stunning theatre design. **Tramway** (tel: 0141-422 2023; www.tramway.org) is an exciting arts centre and theatre space, home of Scottish Ballet.

Below: the Art Deco Glasgow Film Theatre champions arty fare.

Above: the iconic Clyde Auditorium, popularly known as the Armadillo.

The **Tron Theatre** (tel: 0141-552 4267; www.tron.co.uk) shows hard-hitting Scottish drama, concerts, comedy and pantomime. Comedians Billy Connolly and Dave Gorman appear at **The King's Theatre** (tel: 0141-240 1111) in Bath Street and **Pavilion** in Renfield Street (tel: 0870-060 6648).

Scottish Opera and Scottish Ballet mount major productions at the **Theatre Royal** (tel: 0870-060 6647). Modern dance productions, musicals and plays are also staged here.

Classical music and gigs

The **Glasgow Royal Concert Hall** (tel: 0141-353 8000) hosts regular performances by the **Royal Scottish National Orchestra** (tel: 0141-226 3868; www.rsno.org.uk). The refurbished **City Halls** and the **Old Fruit Market** in the Merchant City area are home to the **BBC Scottish Symphony Orchestra** and the Scottish Music Centre (tel: 0141-353 8000). **Henry Wood Hall** (tel: 0141-225 3555; www.rsno.org.uk), at 73 Claremont Street, is a beautiful venue in a former church, mainly used for classical events.

The **Scottish Exhibition and Conference Centre** (tel: 0141-248 3000) and adjacent **Clyde Au-**

ditorium – dubbed the 'Armadillo' – stage high-profile classical concerts and big rock and pop gigs. Jazz, Blues and Country gigs are held at City Halls, Old Fruitmarket and the Royal Concert Hall. For a closer look at Glasgow's music scene and venues see *feature, p.66*.

Film

The first stop for arty, independent film is the wonderful **Glasgow Film Theatre** (12 Rose Street; tel: 0141-332 8128; www.gft.org.uk). Both the **Centre for Contemporary Arts** (**CCA**) and new **Trongate 103** arts centres screen indie films and flicks for kids. For more mainstream releases, try **The Grosvenor** in the West End (Ashton Lane; tel: 0141-339 8444) and the **UGC** multiplex (145–159 West Nile Street; tel: 0870-907 0789).

NIGHTLIFE

Pubs and bars

Drinking has always been a serious business in Glasgow. For sophisticated drinking and eating head to the Merchant City. Sauchiehall Street is mobbed by barefoot stiletto-wielding youth at weekends. The West End is popular with students and arty types.

Some of the best hostelries include **Babbity Bowster** (Mon–Sat 11am–midnight, Sun 12.30pm–midnight) at 16–18 Blackfriars Street, home to a heaving bar that attracts an eclectic mix of media types and local worthies, and **Blackfriars** at 36 Bell Street (daily noon–midnight), which has a friendly bar, a range of real ale beers and is a comedy club and music venue at night. The **Captain's Rest**, at 185 Great Western Road (tel: 0141-332 7304), is great for indie gigs and fun events including Disco Bingo. For Gaelic atmosphere, try **Uisge Beatha**, at 232–246 Woodlands Road (Mon–Sat noon–midnight, Sun 12.30pm–midnight), where the bar staff wear kilts.

Clubs

Glasgow's club scene is eclectic (*see also Gigs, opposite*). **The Arches**, (253 Argyle Street, tel: 0141-565 1000) offers big-name DJs, while **The Buff** (142 Bath Lane, tel: 0141-248 1777) hosts an eclectic mix of music from indie to Motown. **The Flying Duck** (142 Renfield Street, tel: 0141-553 3539) presents indie club nights, oddball cultural gatherings and gigs, and the **Sub Club** (22 Jamaica Street, tel: 0141-248 4600) is the home of the excellent Optimo – rare grooves and stompers for Sunday music hedonists.

F Festivals

Celtic Connections in January celebrates Celtic musical culture. RSNO Proms take place in June. Glasgow International Festival (www.glasgowinternational.org; Apr–May) showcases the latest of Glasgow's cutting-edge visual arts bi-annually. The West End Festival has lots of fun events and concerts in June. The Glasgow Jazz Festival attracts top names in June (www.jazzfest.co.uk).

Glasgow Comedy Festival (www.glasgowcomedyfestival.com) is in March and the arts-orientated Merchant City Festival (www.merchantcityfestival.com) is in September. Glasgay! (tel: 0141-552 7575; www.glasgay.co.uk) in Sept–Nov is Britain's largest gay-lesbian arts festival.

Above: revellers in Ashton Lane at the West End Festival.

High Street

This half-day, 1-mile (1.6km) walk takes you from the gritty old traders' hub Mercat Cross up to the spiritual and spooky realms of the Cathedral area and Necropolis

Mercat Cross was the visible evidence of a burgh's right to hold a market, the domain of traders and merchants, making this area Glasgow's traditional centre of social and economic life for many centuries. There is no clear evidence of where the original **Mercat Cross ❶** stood, and the squat octagonal building with a unicorn-topped pillar which now stands on the intersection at Glasgow Cross is a replacement erected in 1929. The Mercat Building located behind it is, despite its Chicagoesque appearance, a warehouse erected in 1925. The new arts centre Trongate 103 and the Tron theatre (see p.41 for both) are slowly revitalising this part of the Merchant City.

Highlights

- Tolbooth Steeple
- Barony Hall
- Provand's Lordship
- St Mungo Museum of Religious Life and Art
- Cathedral Square and Glasgow Cathedral
- Necropolis

TOLBOOTH STEEPLE

Starting our walk here, the cross is dominated by the **Tolbooth Steeple ❷**, which lies stranded in the middle of busy traffic where the High Street passes into Saltmarket. The Tolbooth was once an integral part of civic life in Glasgow and has occupied this site in

Preceding Pages: Bells Bridge and the 'Armadillo'. **Left:** the Necropolis. **Above:** the Tolbooth Steeple.

various forms since the earliest days. Its functions were manifold, from a meeting place for the town council, to a tax collection point, courthouse and jail.

The square tower was part of a five-storey building which extended west along the Trongate, towards the steeple of **Tron-St Mary's** (see p.41), and its buttressed crown houses the latest of a fine carillon of bells which, in the 18th century, played out a different Scottish melody every two hours. The present bells, installed in 1881, were tended by hereditary bell-ringers, the last of whom, Jessie Herbert, rang the bells until 1970. Their annual high point was, of course, marking the Hogmanay celebrations which saw vast crowds welcoming the New Year in boisterous fashion. The Hogmanay party now takes place in George Square, to the sound of rock bands.

HISTORICAL HIGH STREET

The High Street runs north past Victorian tenements (1883), with shops below on the left and new flats con-

verted from old warehouses on the right. The street names offer clues to the past: Blackfriars Street, from the 13th-century Dominican monastery; Bell Street, after Provost Sir John Bell (1680); and College Street, denoting the **Old College** which was sited here until the middle of the 19th century. The University of Glasgow was established by Bishop William Turnbull in 1451 and flourished for the next few centuries in a pleasant environment between the High Street and the Molendinar Burn. It was here that Adam Smith, author of the seminal work on laissez-faire economics, *The Wealth of Nations*, was appointed Professor of Moral Philosophy in 1752.

The university moved west in 1870 (see p.78), and the site was sold to the City of Glasgow Union Railway Company, which demolished it and erected the College Goods Station, which has now also gone, leaving this area to undergo imminent redevelopment.

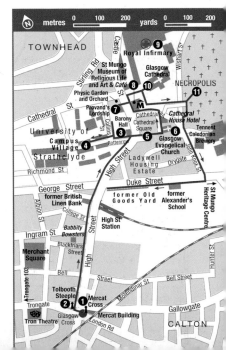

Above: Barony Hall was designed in the Scottish Gothic Revival style and is a popular venue for weddings, as well as the site of graduation ceremonies.

On the left, opposite the High Street Station, is the shell of the old **British Linen Bank**, which has a statue of Pallas, goddess of wisdom and weaving, and a plaque on the corner recalling that the poet Thomas Campbell frequented a coffee shop on the site. Close by, on Nicholas Street, is the College Bar, Glasgow's oldest pub (est. 1515).

Crossing George Street and curving up the hill, the street is flanked by restored tenements with crow-stepped gables, turrets and balconies. On this hill, the Scots freedom fighter William Wallace – glorified by Hollywood and Mel Gibson in the film *Braveheart* – fought a running battle with English forces in 1297.

UNIVERSITY DIGS

On the corner of High Street and Rottenrow is **Barony Hall ❸** (Sat–Sun), the first major building of the Cathedral complex, which opens out onto Castle Street. It was built in 1889 from beautiful red sandstone and graced with slender stained-glass windows and a grey Gothic spire. It is now owned by the University of Strathclyde, and on graduation days the street teems with begowned students and tutors making their way to the hall to receive and bestow degrees. Rottenrow is one of Glasgow's earliest streets, and its name has never been adequately defined,

Below: the Mercat Building *(see p.14)* on the Trongate.

with suggestions as far apart as *route du roi* (king's way) to *vicus ratonum* (street of rats). It leads to the university's **Campus Village** ❹, a pleasing and colourful student quarter built over the past two decades, proving that not all modern architecture is unsympathetic.

AROUND CATHEDRAL SQUARE

Opposite Barony Hall is **Cathedral Square** ❺, guarded by a rather imperious equestrian statue of William of Orange, which was resited by the Provincial Grand Black Chapter of Scotland in 1989 from the Trongate, where it suffered terrible indignities each Hogmanay. It is said that the tail of King Billy's horse was broken off by a reveller and replaced with a ball and socket joint, with the result that on particularly stormy days, the tail can be seen to wave in the breeze.

On the south side of the square is the 1960s Ladywell housing estate, built over the medieval well of that name and the former Duke Street jail. The east side is bounded by the **Glasgow Evangelical Church** ❻, which features life-sized statues of the Apostles. Just to the north, more worldly pleasures can be found at the **Cathedral House**, a small hotel housed in a red sandstone building dating from 1896, which has an interesting three-level bar and is reputedly haunted.

The oldest dwelling-house still standing in Glasgow is **Provand's Lordship** ❼ (tel: 0141-552 8819; www. glasgowmuseums.com; Mon–Thur, Sat 10am–5pm, Fri–Sun 11am–5pm; free). It lies opposite Cathedral Square and was built in 1471 by Bishop Andrew Muirhead to house the master of the hospice of St Nicholas, who looked after a complement of 12 old men.

The house was saved and restored in 1906, with financial aid and period furnishings supplied by Sir William

Above: a sign indicates the oldest Glasgow house still standing, Provand's Lordship, which is now a museum revealing medieval life in the city.

ⓕ Gruesome Tales

If spirits haunt any part of Glasgow, it should be here. Men and women were hanged outside the Tolbooth, and alleged witches and miscreants scourged. The original building had spikes on the walls for the decapitated heads of felons. When the justiciary decamped to the river end of the Saltmarket and the council moved west, the main part of the Tolbooth was lost; only the steeple and its winding stone staircase remain.

Above: the Tolbooth has a long and gruesome history.

Burrell *(see p.88)* in 1927, and is now run by Glasgow Museums. Behind it lies a **Physic Garden**, in tribute to St Nicholas. The sound of the traffic gives way to medieval calm here, among the herb plantings and knot gardens. Behind the wall, towards the Strathclyde campus, is a small but ambitious orchard, where students convene under the spring blossom and try to ignore the M8 just up the road.

RELIGION AND MEDICINE

Back across the High Street – traffic is always bad here – is the **St Mungo Museum of Religious Life and Art** ❽ (tel: 0141-553 2557; www.glasgowmuseums.com; Mon–Sat 10am–5pm, Sun 11am–5pm; free), which caused some controversy before it was opened in 1993 over whether it was an architectural pastiche. The honey-coloured, stone building stands on the site of the medieval Bishop's Castle and houses works of art from the main religions – Buddhist, Christian, Hindu, Jewish, Muslim and Sikh – as well as minor ones. Religious rites are explained alongside intriguing relics and there are gorgeous views from the top floor.

Above: a restored room at Provand's Lordship depicts medieval living.

Inside the Gallery of Religious Art there are powerful images of religious figures and rites to explore including an imposing figure of the Hindu god Shiva, Lord of the Dance, and the Mexican Day of the Dead skeleton, which celebrates the victory of life over death. Illuminating the poignant images are some truly stunning stained-glass windows showing Christian saints and prophets. The museum's pleasant coffee shop backs onto an attractive Zen-style garden

Ⓢ Quirky Shops on the High Street

Along this sweep of handsome red-brick tenements – between the pubs and fish and chip places – there are dishevelled shop fronts aplenty. Among the intriguing and slightly unsettling flavour of shops – from beauty/massage parlours and hair-dressers to religious missions and a butcher or two – there is **23enigma** (258 High Street; tel: 0141-553 1990) which is bubbling with spell books, talismans and crystals. They even offer alternative therapies including hypnosis and reiki.

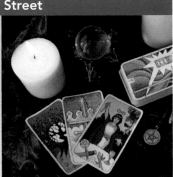

Above: tarot cards are just some of the spooky wares on offer at 23enigma.

Above: the St Mungo Museum of Religious Life and Art has won awards for its fascinating exhibits and attempts to promote inter-faith understanding.

designed by Yasutaro Tanaka, another unexpected haven of peace in this busy street.

The cathedral precinct is fronted by a statue of Scots missionary explorer David Livingstone *(see p.111)* and provides an excellent foreground for the massive bulk of the **Royal Infirmary ❾**, which was completed in 1915 and commemorates the 65-year reign of Queen Victoria, whose solemn presence looms above the entrance. The Royal, which has been operating since 1794, has made a proud contribution to world medicine: Lord Lister pioneered antiseptic surgery here in the 1860s; Sir William Macewen established his reputation in brain surgery and osteopathy here in the 1890s; and his matron Mrs Rebecca Strong introduced the world's first systematic training for nurses. In the early part of the 19th century, its resources were considerably stretched as it sought to cope with epidemics of cholera, typhus

Above: the Royal Infirmary has been the site of many medical breakthroughs.

Above: Barony Chapel, in the crypt of Glasgow Cathedral, is so-named because it was used by Barony parishioners for their worship.

and dysentery. Today, it has one of the busiest casualty departments in Europe, coping with Glasgow's still prevalent weekend bouts of random and inventive violence. One casualty surgeon remarked that it was one of the few cities in Europe where patients still came in with sword wounds.

GLASGOW CATHEDRAL

At the east end of the precinct lies **Glasgow Cathedral** ❿ (tel: 0141-552 8198; Apr–Sept Mon–Sat 9.30am–5pm, Sun 1–5pm, Oct–Mar Mon–Sat 9.30am–4pm, Sun 1–4pm). The tides of history have washed over this important ecclesiastical site since Glasgow's early days. It was founded in 1136 on the site of St Mungo's Church and has always been a focus for Christian learning and culture in Scotland. It has stood through the supremacy of the bishops, the War of Independence and the upheaval of the Reformation, and began to take the shape which

we see today around the middle of the 14th century.

Its blackened stone illustrates the colouring of many Glasgow buildings before stone-cleaning became wide-

Below: Glasgow Cathedral is the best-preserved medieval church in Scotland.

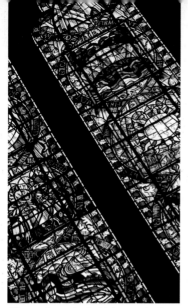

Above: the cathedral is known for its magnificent stained-glass windows.

culture of the operative classes'. The grounds are surrounded by gravestones. Blue-robed custodians belonging to the Society of Friends of Glasgow Cathedral give fascinating little impromptu tours.

Music enthusiasts and anyone interested in the labyrinthine history of this colossal building will be keen to find out about the latest recitals and lectures held in the cathedral. Completing the warm welcome given to visitors and incredible resources available to the curious, there is the Congregations' Library, which is situated in the Cathedral Hall in the basement of the nearby St Mungo Museum *(see p.18)*. It is open on Wednesday afternoons from 2pm to 4pm.

spread. Attempts have been made to clean it up, but it was felt that it would cause too much damage.

The visitors' entrance is flanked by a memorial to the Hutcheson brothers and George Baillie, who 'divested himself of his fortune to endow institutions devoted to the intellectual

Architectural features

The main structure is a rectangle with a cross surmounted by a tower and steeple. A lower church opens up underneath the choir. Damaged by fire, the original cathedral building was succeeded by a larger one, which was consecrated in 1197. Major 13th-century rebuilding by William de Bondinton (1233–58) can be seen in the Quire and the Lower Church.

Ⓕ St Mungo

Legend has it that a century after St Ninian dedicated a Christian burial ground at Cathures (later Glasgow) Kentigern arrived, popularly known as Mungo. Kentigern hailed from Culross in Fife (Glaswegians may be taken aback to learn that their patron saint was in fact a Fifer) where he was trained as a priest by St Serf. He accompanied the corpse of a holy man, Fergus – carried on a cart by two oxen – to the St Ninian's burial ground in Cathures where Fergus was buried.

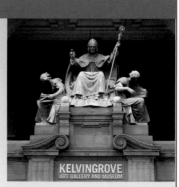

Above: images of St Mungo, Glasgow's patron saint, adorn the city.

Check out the doorways of the sacristy (Upper Chapterhouse) and of the Lower Chapterhouse; these date from the mid-13th century. Extensive work enlarged the nave in the 14th century – for a closer look at these developments seek out the southwest door and the entrance to the Blacader Aisle, where the body of Fergus is said to have been buried by St Mungo (see box p.21).

Other intriguing architectural and social developments occurred after the Reformation to allow three different congregations to worship in different spaces, reflecting rank and class divisions. From 1595, the Barony Parishioners worshipped in the lower church (crypt), while from 1648 the High Kirk congregation worshipped in the choir itself, and the nave was used by worshippers from the eastern part of the city. Ask one of the robed custodians for interesting tidbits from this period.

NECROPOLIS

At the south side of the Cathedral is a bridge which spans Wishart Street and leads to the **Necropolis** ⓫ (7am–dusk; free) an impressive ornamental garden cemetery modelled on Père-Lachaise in Paris. It is full of crumbling temples and monuments, many of which are in a sorry state of repair, which only adds to the chilling atmosphere, especially on dreich days.

In 1831, John Strang, Chamberlain at the Merchants' House, wrote *Necropolis Glasguensis*, or 'Thoughts on Death and Moral Stimulus', which included an outline of city plans for the hilly parkland site, previously known as Fir Park, which he considered to

ⓥ Views Between the Tombs

The views of the Cathedral from the hill housing the Necropolis not only give some idea of the imposing grandeur of the Cathedral in medieval times, but also afford superb vistas as far as Ben Lomond to the north-west and the Cathkin Braes to the south. Roe deer can be seen roaming between the monument obelisks and haughty headstones. The combination of wildlife and monumental Victorian display and decay – with a skyline backdrop of lines of high-rise flats and churches – is strangely spine-tingling.

Above: situated on a hill, the Necropolis offers wonderful views.

Above: crumbling memorials in the Victorian Necropolis.

appear 'admirably adapted for a Pere la Chaise, which would harmonise beautifully with the adjacent scenery, and constitute a solemn and appropriate appendage to the venerable structure (the Cathedral) in front of which, while it will afford a much wanted accommodation to the higher classes, would at the same time con-

Below: a Celtic cross adorns a grave in the Necropolis.

vert an unproductive property into a general and lucrative source of profit, to a charitable institution'. It was to be 'respectful to the dead, safe and sanitary to the living, dedicated to the Genius of Memory and to extend religious and moral feeling'.

Architect David Hamilton, Stuart Murray, Curator of the Botanic Gardens, and James Clelland, Superintendent of Public Works, produced a feasibility study for forming the Glasgow Necropolis, and in 1828 the committee of Directors of Lands and Quarries agreed to the proposal. Then in 1831, a competition for converting the Fir Park into a cemetery was launched, with five prizes up for grabs of £10–50. As the burial ground was intended to be interdenominational, the first burial in 1832 was fittingly that of a Jew, Joseph Levi, a jeweller. Extensions into quarry ground in the 1860s and 1870s give us the present-day dimensions of 37 acres (15 hectares).

A walk around the graves

Some 50,000 burials have taken place at the Necropolis and most of the 3,500 tombs are about 14ft (4m)

Above: one of the Necropolis's elaborate tombs.

deep, with solid stone walls and brick partitions. Some of the Necropolis tombs on the top of the hill were blasted out of the rock face. Many of the monuments were designed by major architects and sculptors, including Alexander 'Greek' Thomson, Charles Rennie Mackintosh and J.T.

Below: a stone angel on one of the Necropolis's monuments.

Rochead, which makes a walk around the sprawling site a fascinating insight into Victorian and Edwardian styles and tastes. The administration and maintenance of the Necropolis was handed from Merchants' House to Glasgow City Council in 1966.

The Necropolis's grand bridge was built by the Merchants' House of Glasgow to 'afford a proper entrance to the new cemetery combining convenient access to the grounds' and views of 'the venerable Cathedral and surrounding scenery'. Paths lead in circles round the hill past gloomy, ivy-clad, marble-pillared tombs and sombre obelisks. The Victorians took themselves as seriously in death as in life. The crowning monument on the summit is to John Knox, the austere father of the Reformation in Scotland, which 'produced a revolution in the sentiments of mankind'. Knox still keeps a suspicious eye on the city below. The Friends of Glasgow Necropolis (www.glasgow necropolis.org) is a superb organisation which runs tours of the site and various cultural events.

BACK TO GLASGOW CROSS

Leaving the cemetery in Wishart Street, this tour continues past the huge steel tanks of the **Tennent Caledonian Brewery**, which supplies a commodity as welcome to many Glaswegians as Loch Katrine's water. At the foot of the street the modern flats and high-rise blocks on the right stand on the site of the Drygate, one of the original streets of old Glasgow.

Turning right into Duke Street, past the former Alexander's School, now a business centre (adorned with busts of the heads of Shakespeare and other luminaries on its frontage), the road follows along the wall of the old College Goods Yard.

To return to Glasgow Cross, turn left at the traffic lights and head into the High Street.

Above: the tanks of the Tennent Caledonian Brewery stand in close proximity to the Necropolis tombs.

E Eating Out

Babbity Bowsters
16–18 Blackfriars Street; tel: 0141-552 5055; daily lunch and dinner. Housed in a handsome Adam brothers-designed building, this popular hangout has the Schottische restaurant serving hearty portions of Scottish classic dishes with a Gallic twist here and there. The homely pub serves decent ales and malts to a live folk music soundtrack. This place is popular with a diverse crowd. £

St Mungo Museum Café
St Mungo Museum of Religious Life and Art; Mon–Sat 10am–5pm, Sun 11am–5pm.
This museum café serves predominantly simple, honest British grub, as well as some pasta dishes, heaped salads and good-value soup of the day. There is also an attractive garden where you can enjoy your meal in good weather.

Above: Babbity Bowsters.

Tour 2

The Barras to Saltmarket

This short 2-mile (3.2km) walk explores the banter and bargains of the Barras, Glasgow Green's delights and a short stroll south to the Clyde

If the High Street walk *(see p.14)* un-covers layers of Glasgow's history, this tour, which takes in the lively Bar-ras, is where the city's working class past meets modern struggles and endeavours. This walk is a real eye-opener and bound to deliver some memorable, oddball stories, encoun-ters and scenes.

Although at first glance this busy marketplace is tatty and run-down, the area is full of life and colour, and bargain-hunters flock to it from all over the city and beyond. Down towards the Clyde and over the bridge there are old and new popular Glaswegian institutions – including the People's Palace museum and the handsome Winter Gardens at Glasgow Green – as well as the Citizens Theatre and

Highlights

- The Saracen's Head
- Exploring the Barras
- The People's Palace
- Glasgow Green
- Doulton Fountain
- St Andrew's Parish Church
- Central Mosque
- Citizens Theatre
- Clyde Walkway
- Saltmarket

Central Mosque. Round the corner from historic folk music pubs there are notorious locations etched on the Glaswegian psyche, like Nelson's Pillar, sight of many a public hanging.

Left: one of the riverside developments on the banks of the Clyde. **Above:** the Central Mosque *(see p.34)*.

Saturday or Sunday are the best days to undertake this tour, as the majority of shops around the Saltmarket are open.

ALONG GALLOWGATE

Starting the walk from the **Mercat Cross** *(see p.14)*, head east up the **Gallowgate**, which is generally accepted to have the macabre meaning

its name implies. However, the late historian George Eyre-Todd suggested that it meant the *gait*, or way to, the *gia lia*, or sacred stone of Celtic times, which would make it one of the oldest roads in Scotland. Social raconteur Jack House recalls days in the 1930s when the street housed 60 pubs and he 'never ventured there without an occasional *frisson* disturbing me'.

The road leads under a bridge, passing a row of discount shops, as well as Moir Street and Charlotte Street, after which you reach Glasgow's oldest chippie (1884) at Little Dovehill and then Great Dovehill on the left. According to legend, this is where St Mungo was preaching to his flock when someone at the back complained that he could not see him, whereupon he commanded the adjoining ground to rise up in the air.

A little further along, you will come to **The Saracen's Head ❶** (Sat 11am–11pm, Sun 12.30–11pm), or 'The Sarry Heid', a pub whose glory days are most definitely behind it. It lays claim to being the first real hotel in Glasgow, built in 1755 from the ruins of the old bishop's castle, and takes its name from a 12th-century

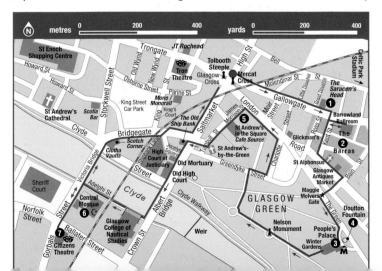

Above: The Barras market takes its name from the Glaswegian dialect for 'barrow'; in the market's early years, the traders sold their goods from handcarts.

inn in London frequented by Richard the Lionheart. The first mail coach from London arrived here in 1788, and it was a haunt of Scotland's judges as they progressed round the western circuit from Edinburgh.

THE BARRAS

Crossing the road to Kent Street, **The Barras** ❷ (Sat–Sun 10am–5pm) originated as a street market consisting of hand-barrows hired out by the McIver family to traders too poor to have their own. The covered market

came into being in 1926 and, after a spell in the doldrums in the 1970s and 1980s, it has been revitalised and is now said to be one of the biggest markets in Europe.

Second-hand furniture and clothes predominate, although in keeping with the times, DVDs, computer games and CDs, whose legality is continually challenged by trading standards officers, now feature. Slightly further along the Gallowgate from the Kent Street entrance is the **Barrowland Ballroom**, a dance

❻ Sarry Heid's Colourful Patrons and Relics

The old inn has been visited by an impressive list of patrons, including Robert Burns, John Wesley, James Boswell, William Wordsworth and Adam Smith, who was allegedly ejected after a swearing match with Dr Samuel Johnson. It houses the 1760 Saracen's Head punchbowl and the skull of Maggie, the last witch to be burned at the stake, which the title deeds demand is to be passed to the People's Palace if the pub is ever demolished.

Glasgow's first
PUB - MUSEUM ☠
See the Skull of Maggie the last witch to be burned at the stake. Read a poem in Rabbie Burns' ane handwriting.

Above: the Sarry Heid's inn displays a range of quirky artefacts.

Above: the Barrowland Ballroom is a popular venue with a variety of local and high-profile international acts, who praise the acoustics and atmosphere.

hall which was the focus of the 1960s Bible John murders – when three women were killed by a man with a penchant for quoting Old Testament texts to his victims – but is now one of Glasgow's largest live music venues, staging gigs by local bands like Camera Obscura and international stars, including one of Dumbarton's finest sons, David Byrne.

In case you are wondering about the green-and-white-striped men often seen staggering along the Gallowgate, chanting musical ditties, these are fans of Celtic Football Club. Among the many bars to and from **Celtic Park Stadium**, a 15-minute walk east of the Barras, is Baird's Bar, next door to the Barrowland

Ballroom. It is a well-known Hoops haunt and pre-gig watering hole. Pop your head in to see an eye-opening afternoon karaoke session, or if you are on the way to a game at Paradise, Celtic's home ground (for fixtures and tickets go to www.celticfc.net), this is a good spot to soak up some local banter and gauge the mood of the local support.

Kent Street leads through to London Road, and, turning left, you'll see St Alphonsus Church. Next door is **Glasgow Antiques Market** (tel: 0141-552 6989; Sat–Sun 9.30am–4.30pm), which has a café attached. Proceed down Bain Street, through the Maggie McIvers Gate, and into **Glasgow Green**. Through the trees you will see the exotic coloured-brick frontage of the old Templeton's carpet factory, an enthusiastic copy of the Doge's Palace in Venice, designed by William Leiper in 1889. The factory is now a business centre.

PEOPLE'S PALACE

Turn left for the **People's Palace** ❸ (tel: 0141-276 0788; www.glasgow museums.com; Mon–Thur and Sat 10am–5pm, Fri and Sun 11am–5pm; free), a museum presiding over one

Left: shopping for fruit and veg at the Barras; a farmers' market is also held here on the last Saturday of the month.

of the tree-lined avenues of Glasgow Green and a favourite with Glaswegians. It was built as a cultural centre for workers in 1898, who were living in some of the most abject conditions of the Industrial age. Lord Rosebery outlined the purpose of the grandiose civic project: 'A palace of pleasure and imagination around which the people may place their affections and which may give them a home on which their memory may rest'. He then declared the building as 'Open to the people for ever and ever'.

Originally, the ground floor provided space for reading and recreation, with a museum on the first floor, and a picture gallery on the top floor. Since the 1940s it has concentrated on the history and the way of life of the working class as well as kings and cardinals. Exhibits range from a ring which belonged to Mary, Queen of Scots to comedian Billy Connolly's 'banana boots'. The red-sandstone building, with its domed roof and pillared frontage, was completely refurbished for its centenary in 1998 and now uses the latest computer technology and film to tell its story.

Above: an exotic and colourful flower at the Winter Gardens.

On the top floor is a powerful series of paintings by artist and Glasgow School of Art graduate Ken Currie, who was commissioned to mark the 1987 bicentenary of the massacre of Glasgow's Calton weavers, Scotland's first trade union martyrs. The series of eight paintings adorns the splendid dome: the cycle begins in 1787 and ends with a vision of the future. It traces the development of the Scottish labour move-

Above: the Winter Gardens hosts exhibitions and events throughout the year.

Above: the Winter Gardens café is a pleasant place to spend some time, particularly on a cold or rainy day.

ment through Currie's powerful imagery. **The Winter Gardens** (daily 10am–5pm), a huge conservatory housing tropical palms and ferns, butts onto the back of the Palace. After a serious fire in January 1998, it has now reopened and houses a café-cum-bar.

GLASGOW GREEN

In 1450 Bishop Turnbull gave the common lands of **Glasgow Green** to the people of the city, although its previously rural vista is now bounded by the high-rise flats of the Gorbals, across the river. Bonnie Prince Charlie mustered his armies here, and the Glasgow Fair, instituted in 1190, is still celebrated in the park in the last fortnight of July. Turning right past the palace, a 144ft (44m) needle erected to commemorate Lord Nelson dominates the western end.

In front of the People's Palace, the magnificent red-terracotta **Doulton Fountain ❹**, gifted by the Victorian china manufacturer to commemorate Queen Victoria's Golden Jubilee of 1887, has recently been restored with National Lottery Fund money. Its five-tier, 46ft (14m) -high and 70ft (21m) -wide display of imperial pride makes

it the largest terracotta fountain in the world and a mesmerising insight into Glasgow's prominent place in the British Empire. It was first unveiled at the Empire Exhibition held at Kelvingrove Park in 1888 and then moved to Glasgow Green in 1890. Take a

Ⓚ Giant Productions

Along Saltmarket, amid the curious array of shops, is the HQ of Giant Space (121–127 Saltmarket; tel: 0141-552 8231; www.giantprod uctions.org), a cultural organisation dedicated to kids' drama, visual arts, music, theatre, storytelling and puppetry. Check out the website and see local press for upcoming events staged all over town.

Above: Giant Productions promotes inspiring arts experiences for kids.

Above: the splendid People's Palace and Doulton Fountain on Glasgow Green.

walk around it to get a closer look at extravagant figurative groups representing India, Australia, Canada and South Africa. Seek out national flora and fauna (South Africa's ostrich, Australian sheep and Canadian beaver), alongside military and naval figures including a kilted highlander. Completing the dizzying decorations are gargoyles, coats of arms, lion masks, and young girls pouring water over the figures below. Topping the whole

Ⓢ Independent Shopping

It may have the Barras and some scruffy old markets, but this area is not renowned for its upmarket shopping. However, a few excellent independent shops and specialist outlets have opened in recent years which are well worth seeking out. **Monorail** (12 Kings Court, King Street; tel: 0141-552 9458; Mon–Sat 11am–7pm, Sun noon–5pm) is run by Pastels front man Stephen Pastel, and is a must for musos and vinyl addicts. They have a great vegan-friendly café and a space for cultural events, cinema screenings and other cultural get-togethers.

Just north of Monorail is Glasgow's best comic shop, **A1 Comics** (35 Parnie Street; tel: 0141-552 6692; daily 9.30am–5.30pm, Sun noon–5pm), which has some fine toys for kids and objects for geeky adults alongside piles of Marvel and DC editions. Just off the London Road is **GOOD:D** (11 James Morrison Street; tel: 0141-552 6777; daily 9.30am–5.30pm, Sun noon–5pm), which is full of quirky modern design pieces.

Above: the music shop Monorail is heaven for vinyl lovers.

Above: Nelson's Pillar (1806) was the first civic monument in Britain to commemorate the Admiral's victories.

Imperial enterprise is a lifelike statue of Queen Victoria.

ST ANDREW'S IN THE SQUARE

Returning north to London Road, along Charlotte Street, is Glickman's fabulous confectionery shop (est. 1903), a sweet-tooth's paradise. The tour continues towards Glasgow Cross and left into James Morrison Street and St Andrew's Square, which houses **St Andrew's Parish Church ⑤** (now known as St Andrew's in the Square), the oldest church in the city after the Cathedral. It was modelled on St Martin-in-the-Fields in London, and its massive pillars and stone ornamentation illustrate the grand tastes of the 18th-century Tobacco Lords. It now stages musical and other cultural events, and houses the excellent Café Source *(see p.37)*.

The south side of the square passes the district courts, where minor offenders are daily chastised, and, turning left and then right into Steel Street, the route leads to the Saltmarket. The pub on the facing corner, **The Old Ship Bank**, recalls the first Glasgow bank, set up in 1750 to meet the needs of the influential and rising merchant class. Going left down the Saltmarket, the new **High Court of Justiciary** extension is tucked into Jocelyn Square behind the old Mortuary. Further along is the old High Court, with its forbidding grey-pillared portico, which has seen the black cap donned for a procession of murderers. It fronted onto Jail Square, where the guilty were hanged before cheering crowds in the shadow of Nelson's Pillar, giving rise to the maternal Glaswegian warning to recalcitrant children: 'You'll die facing the monument.'

TOWARDS AND OVER THE CLYDE

Saltmarket runs down onto the **Albert Bridge**, or Hutchesontown Bridge, a cast-iron structure built in 1871 on enormous granite piers on the site of a crossing first created in

Above: St Andrew's in the Square has been restored to its 18th-century glory.

Above: inside the Citizens Theatre.

1794. Just upstream is the weir which marks the tidal limit of the river and controls its natural vagaries. Over the bridge, appropriately at the river's junction with the sea, is the **Glasgow College of Nautical Studies**, festooned with lifeboats, survival craft, radar and masts.

Turning right onto the south bank of the river at the start of the college, a tree-lined walkway leads to the peaceful colonnaded grounds of the **Central Mosque** ❻ (tel: 0141-429 3132; www.centralmosque.co.uk; daily 9am–5pm for visitors, booking essential; 24 hours for prayers), which in 1984 became the first purpose-built mosque in Scotland and is now one of the largest in Europe. Its green, multi-faceted dome and soaring minaret contrast with the 1960s architecture of the surrounding Gorbals blocks. It provides the facilities of worship for 2,000 Muslims, a community whose numbers have increased dramatically in the 1980s and 1990s and who now play an integral part in city life.

The forbidding black-and-grey-marbled building on the other side of Gorbals Street is the **Sheriff Court** where solicitors gather to ply an ancient trade. It moved here when the old, smaller, city-centre court became unable to cope with the numbers that make it the busiest court in Europe.

Further south down Gorbals Street, across the junction with Ballater Street, is the **Citizens Theatre** ❼ (tel: 0141-429 0022; www.citz.co.uk), a cornerstone of Glasgow's artistic life and a major contributor to its ambition to be considered as a European city. The Citizen's Company was es-

Above: the Albert Bridge.

Ⓖ Clyde Walkway

This 40-mile (65km) -long path is being developed to link Glasgow with the Falls of Clyde at Lanark. Cyclists and walkers will particularly enjoy the Glasgow section between Victoria Bridge and the SECC, which passes the PS *Waverley* Terminal – home of the world's last sea-going paddle steamer – and the colossal 176ft (53m) -high Finnieston Crane, which once raised railway locomotives. There are a number of other long-distance paths that link with the Clyde Walkway, including the Kelvin Walkway, the Glasgow to Inverness National Cycle Route, and paths to Edinburgh, Greenock and Irvine.

Above: see ongoing riverside development from the Clyde Walkway.

tablished in 1943 amid a row of Gorbals tenements, in a grand Victorian building originally called His Majesty's Theatre, which had been opened in 1878. Scottish playwright James Bridie drove the project as part of a plan to establish a Scottish national theatre. It drifted from drama into crisis until the arrival in 1969 of director Giles Havergal and his flamboyant designer Philip Prowse. Their ground-breaking productions – sometimes shocking and disturbing – attracted headlines and interest far beyond Glasgow and continue to fill the hall. The theatre houses a main auditorium and two small studio theatres which offer cutting-edge works.

Above: the green dome of the Central Mosque against the Gorbals tower blocks.

Above: St Andrew's Cathedral is striking amongst the modern riverside buildings.

HEADING BACK NORTH OF THE CLYDE

Returning along Gorbals Street, the road comes to **Victoria Bridge**, where the city's first river crossing, a wooden structure commissioned by Bishop Rae in 1350, stood for 450 years. The present bridge is faced with Dublin granite and affords excel-

Below: the Clutha Vaults pub is renowned for its live acoustic and folk music and is a real Glasgow institution.

lent views down river past the Carlton Place Suspension Bridge to the Jamaica Street and Central Station bridges. The Gothic-spired building on the north bank is **St Andrew's Cathedral** (www.cathedralg1.org; closed for renovation until late 2010), the main Roman Catholic church, which is reflected in the modern glass-walled diocesan headquarters next door. The glass pyramids rising above the rooftops behind it are the canopies of the St Enoch shopping centre. The Clyde Walkway, a riverside promenade, is slowly taking shape, bringing the river back into the heart of Glasgow by steadily reviving the fortunes of a long-depressed riverfront with new hotels and apartments.

Across the bridge on the north bank, two adjoining pubs, the **Clutha Vaults** and the **Scotch Corner** (both 11am–midnight), may look a tad scruffy from the outside but are a focus for the folk circuit. Above these pubs is the three-tiered spire of the old fish market, topped with a golden sailing ship. Nearby, the Scotia Bar at 112–114 Stockwell Street stages folk acts as well as poetry and literary events.

Under the railway bridge, on waste ground between St Margaret's Place and the new High Court buildings, is where **Paddy's Market** was held until May 2009. The old defunct market had its origins, as the name suggests, in the floods of refugees from the Irish potato famine. Labelled a 'crime-ridden midden' by the council, the area is set to be transformed into a new cultural quarter to link up with the exciting new artsy venues and bars on the Trongate and Merchant City *(see p.40)*. Some residents have not taken too kindly to the attempt to gentrify the area, but most see the benefits of encouraging new initiatives to clean up and hopefully transform squalor into a bustling centre of arts and enterprise.

Turning left at the end of the Briggait, the **Saltmarket** – so-named because the original market for salt for curing river salmon was sited here – curves back up to the High Street past restored tenements and busy shops.

A NEW CULTURAL QUARTER

Veering right into the Bridgegate, or Briggait, one of Glasgow's oldest streets, this tour passes second-hand shops, cheap restaurants and the expanse of the King Street car park.

🄴 Eating Out

Café Source
1 St Andrew's Square; tel: 0141-559 5902; daily lunch and dinner.
Locally sourced ingredients go into the hearty fare served in the basement of St Andrew's in the Square. £

JT Rochead
60 Trongate; tel: 0141-548 1350; daily lunch and dinner.
Hidden in the back of the busy Maggie's Bar on the Trongate, this intimate place concentrates on traditional Scots fare with some imaginative additions. Standouts include salmon with thyme-infused gnocchi and apple crumble with vanilla ice cream. £

Mono
12 King's Court, King Street; tel: 0141-553 2400; www.monocafebar.com; Sun–Thur noon–8pm, Fri–Sat noon–10pm; bar noon–midnight, noon–1am Fri–Sat.

A popular music and arts venue with a great record shop, Mono squeezes in a café with a vegan menu. Top dishes include the falafel platter served with vegetables and hummous, and the Mono veggie burger. £

Above: Café Source offers a range of traditional and modern Scottish fare.

Sandstone & Steel

Roads, slum clearances, high-rise schemes and recession may have savaged the city in the past, but Glasgow's innovative spirit is reinvigorating the urban landscape of the future

SOLID SANDSTONE SPIRIT

In Glasgow's city centre, grand drama and extravagance in sculpted stone predominates.

From the weathered 13th-century remnants found in the vicinity of Glasgow Cathedral and the 17th-century mercantile optimism around the Trongate, to the grandeur of the mansions of the Tobacco Lords in the Merchant City in the 18th century and the robust flowering of the Victorians in the British Empire's heyday, Glasgow developed into a city carved painstakingly from sandstone.

Although Charles Rennie Mackintosh (see Tour 9) and Alexander 'Greek' Thomson are foremost in the current view of Glasgow's architectural heritage, others such as William Young – who created the City Chambers as a monument to civic pride in 1888 – J.T. Rochead, J.J. Burnet and Charles Wilson all contributed mightily. Rochead's work in St Vincent Street sets the tone for the commercial centre, and his Grosvenor Hotel is a true Venetian marvel, Burnet's former TSB banking hall on the corner of Ingram Street and Glassford Street

tions like James Miller's miniature version of France's Azay-le-Rideau in the centre of St Enoch Square.

GLASS, STEEL AND THE FUTURE

Modern architecture in Glasgow is following a bold tradition. Atlantic Quay on the Clyde has waterfront grandeur, as does the Clyde Auditorium (dubbed the Armadillo for its distinctive shape) by Sir Norman Foster. The Glasgow Science Centre complex has titanium curves and a soaring viewing tower, called the Titan. The open-plan interior of the new BBC Scotland building on Pacific Quay is equally bold; so, too, is the Clyde Arc Bridge.

Visionary projects taking shape include the striking Riverside Museum, designed by Zaha Hadid, with its wave-like 'pleated' aluminium shapes, and the new Glasgow School of Art Garnethill Estate redevelopment, opposite Mackintosh's architectural masterpiece. In September 2009, Steven Holl Architects' (New York) light-filled design won a high-profile competition to build the GSA's new teaching and research centre.

Other recent projects have imaginatively adapted some of Glasgow's old sandstone architecture. To the innovative renovations at the Italian Centre, Tron Theatre and Princes Square, can be added Trongate 103, a cutting-edge arts hub hewn out of an Edwardian warehouse. It's all part of Glasgow City Council's plan to regenerate this part of the Merchant City, down to the River Clyde, and in doing so, creating an enlarged cultural quarter.

A great way to absorb Glasgow's architecture is on a guided tour. For information about Glasgow Architectural Walking Tours, including a visit to the GSA, check out www.glasgow architecture.co.uk.

outshines the bigger surroundings, while Wilson created an Italianate skyscape in the Park Circus area unequalled in Britain.

Huge enterprises like Robert Anderson's Central Hotel and the Edwardian mass of the Royal Technical College (now the University of Strathclyde) vie for attention with small-scale confec-

Above: Tradeston Bridge in Atlantic Quay, nicknamed 'squiggly' because of its S-shaped design. **Top Left**: the Glasgow Tower, part of the Science Centre complex and the tallest tower in Scotland. **Centre Left**: classic Glaswegian sandstone architecture. **Left**: Charles Rennie Mackintosh.

Merchant City

From Trongate's vibrant new arts centres, this half-day ¾-mile (1.2km) walk delves into the heart of the Merchant City's cool hangouts, conversions and enterprising institutions

The Merchant City fell into decline during the 1980s recession, leaving huge warehouses abandoned and businesses boarded up. Ambitious developments and stylish conversions, added to visionary arts projects, including the Tron Theatre and Trongate 103, have brought the area back to life. Expect an earthy mix of arty creativity and working-class wit.

While other cities have wrestled with inner-city problems, Glasgow perversely had an outer-city problem. Huge schemes – Drumchapel, Easterhouse, Castlemilk and Pollok, which were created after World War II to facilitate slum clearance – stand guard at each corner of the boundaries. In the late 1970s and early 1980s, Glasgow was tagged

Highlights

- Tron Theatre
- Trongate 103
- Old Fruit Market
- Ramshorn Kirk and Cemetery
- City Halls
- Old Glasgow Sheriff Court
- Hutchesons' Hall
- Italian Centre
- Trades Hall

Doughnut City – plenty round the outside and nothing in the middle. The Merchant City was Glasgow's attempt to bring life back to the central warehouse district. The square-mile area is now home to a core of

Left: the Glasgow Jazz Festival is held at the Old Fruit Market (see p.42).
Above: the stylish new Trongate 103.

young professionals and arty types. The blend of old and new architecture creates an exciting fusion which is echoed in the many restaurants offering innovative cross-cultural food. Alongside exciting new arts developments including the Tron Theatre and Trongate 103 there's a wealth of pubs, clubs and independent shops. Keep your eyes peeled on partnership plans with Glasgow City Council for the Merchant City's next phase of arts-led regeneration, which is heading south of the Trongate, to create a cultural quarter down to the Clyde (see p.39).

ALONG THE TRONGATE

Starting the route at the old heart of the city at **Mercat Cross** (see p.14), go west along the Trongate. The tenements along each side date from the middle and end of the 19th century, and their rich facades funnel the street along to an almost Central European steeple whose base is an open arch across the busy pavement. This is **Tron-St Mary's**, a former church, and, like the street, is named after the weighing machine, or tron, introduced by the Bishop of Glasgow in 1491 to weigh and tax goods coming into the city. The church has been operating as the **Tron Theatre** ❶ (tel: 0141-552 4267; www.tron.co.uk) since 1982, first as a club, and since 1990 it has been a full public venue. The Tron Theatre features a programme of both contemporary and traditional Scottish drama, and its restaurant – which offers cracking lunchtime and pre-theatre menus – is a popular meeting place.

Continuing west along the Trongate you come to the impressive **Trongate 103** ❷ (tel: 0141-287 9835; www.trongate103.com; Mon–Sat 10am–5pm, Sun noon–5pm), a massive Edwardian warehouse converted into an exciting arts centre, which opened in 2009. Beyond the cavernous contemporary atrium – imaginatively hewn out of the old handsome red-sandstone warehouse – are five floors of print studios, retail shops and galleries, where artists and the public can mingle and exchange ideas (see box p.43).

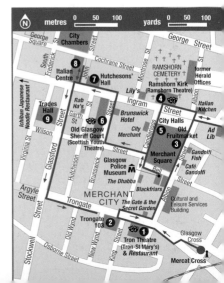

Above: exploring the Trongate, the old centre of the city.

UP ALBION STREET AND THE OLD FRUITMARKET

Crossing Trongate, head back eastwards then up Albion Street, past a magnificent red-sandstone bas-relief on the Cultural and Leisure Services building on the right, to the junction with Bell Street. This intersection has more pubs than the rest of both long streets put together. On the left, **Blackfriars** is large and lively, with a basement which hosts live music nights; **Café Gandolfi**, on the right, was one of the original Merchant City restaurants and contains the fantastical wood furniture of Tim Stead. **Gandolfi Fish**, an excellent seafood haunt, is just a few doors along. There are lots of lively pubs and restaurants which occupy various old buildings including the **Old Fruitmarket** ❸.

The fruit market moved from its former congested home here in 1969 and now nestles, with the fishmarket, beside the M8 at Blochairn. The south end housed a successful general market for many years before closing to accommodate the new pubs. The north end, however, lay closed

for years, until enthusiasts from the performing arts section of the council realised that its cobbled streets and balconied offices, which used to ring to the iron wheels of carts and the shouts of traders, would make an ideal, New Orleans-style venue for the annual

Above: Café Gandolfi has been serving for 25 years and is known for its good food and stylish interior.

Above: the Old Fruit Market packs lots of period charm under its vaulted roof.

Glasgow Jazz Festival. The extensively refurbished Old Fruitmarket is a much-loved performance space and hosts regular events and parties.

The building above the excellent **Italian Kitchen** pizzeria and café, where Albion Street crosses Ingram Street, housed the original Mitchell Library collection on two floors in 1877. Stephen Mitchell came from a tobacco family and left a huge estate to provide books 'on all subjects not immoral' for the edification of the city's working classes. His initiative was the impetus

Ⓕ Scots and International Arts at Trongate 103

Resident organisations at Trongate 103 include the Russian Cultural Centre and Café Cosachock, Glasgow Print Studio, Street Level Photoworks, Transmission Gallery, Glasgow Project Room and Project Ability. Don't miss a journey into the darkly magic world of wonders and nuances of the Sharmanka (Russian for hurdy gurdy) Kinetic Theatre. This atmospheric space chimes with the workings of Edward Bersudsky and Tatyana Jakovskaya's fantastical inventions: a mesmerising, gently unfolding whirl of mechanical finds, *objets trouvés* and sculptural inventions, accompanied by crackly old Eastern European music.

Above: artworks for perusal at the Glasgow Print Studio.

for the public library service; today, the
Mitchell Library (see p.63) is the largest
public reference library in Europe.

On the opposite corner, Greenwich
Village-style loft apartments are situated in a former Strathclyde University building. Further up Albion Street,
the four-storey black-glass office formerly housed *The Herald* newspaper, which prides itself on being the
world's oldest English-language daily.
The newspaper has moved to offices
in the city centre and the old offices
are to be turned into flats.

INGRAM STREET AND
THE RAMSHORN

Looking right along Ingram Street,
the **Ad Lib** bar/diner (tel: 0141-
552 5736) on the right-hand side is
housed in a red-sandstone building
with a splendid coat of arms over the
entrance. This was the Central Fire
Station, built in 1899, and the home

of Wallace the Fire Dog, the mascot
who faithfully escorted the engines
on their dangerous missions. The en-
gine room used to contain a memorial to the 19 firemen who died in the
Cheapside Street whisky bond blaze
in 1960, an event which still scars the
memory of many families in the city.

As you turn left along Ingram Street,
the **Ramshorn Kirk** ❹ looms out
of a grove of unlikely urban elms. The
Gothic church with its square clock
tower is properly known as St David's
(Ramshorn) and was built in 1824 on
the Ramshorn estate. Thomas Rick-
man, a Birmingham architect, was
chosen to design the present building
upon the site of an 18th-century 'God
Box'-style church. Its alluring design is
based on a late 13th- and 14th-century
Gothic design. Those tall and narrow,
beautifully proportioned dimensions,
soaring stained-glass windows, and
substantial crypt show all the hall-

ⓢ Retail Therapy

The Merchant City has swanky boutiques and foodie places aplenty. **Boudiche** (203 Ingram Street; tel: 0845-475 0250) stocks chic lingerie labels including Stella McCartney and Christian Lacroix. If it's jewellery you're after, head to **Brazen** (8 Albion Street; tel: 0141-552 4551) where you'll find unique pieces by independent designers and cool watches by Lip. If your tummy is rumbling, go to **Peckham's** (61–65 Glassford Street; tel: 0141-553 0666), a superb deli with a fine selection of cheeses, wines, beers and gourmet treats downstairs, a sleek ground-floor café and a cooking school upstairs (see p.119).

Above: Peckham's sells delicious delicatessen goodies.

marks of Gothic Revival Scots Style. It is built in handsome blond sandstone mined from a nearby quarry at Cowcaddens, and its tower – towards the front of the building – is 120ft (36m) high and houses a set of bells which have never been rung. The building is now used by the Strathclyde University Theatre Group, which stages an eclectic repertoire in the small performance space (see local press for details) and uses the crypt as rehearsal rooms. The intimate, atmospheric space is well worth visiting, especially for a performance.

The **Ramshorn Cemetery** is a verdant respite from street noise and a fascinating voice from the past. Many gravestones are so old as to be illegible, and some are still barred and spiked against the predations of grave robbers. Emile L'Angelier, arsenic victim of the infamous Madeleine Smith, is buried here, as is David Dale, philanthropic co-founder of New Lanark, and John 'Phosphorus' Anderson, the ebullient father of Strathclyde University. On the pavement outside,

worn by thousands of careless feet, are the initials R.F. and A.F., marking the resting place of the Foulis brothers, a pair of enterprising and painstaking printers who perfected the craft for Glasgow University in the 18th century. Robert Foulis was also instrumental in establishing an Academy of Arts some 14 years before the Royal Academy in London.

CITY HALLS AND CANDLERIGGS

The Ramshorn stands sentinel at the head of Candleriggs, a street which takes its name from the noisome candleworks which initially operated well away from the main population. This is the heart of the Merchant City, with coffee houses and fashionable bars on the right and the substantially refurbished **City Halls** ❺, where Dickens drew crowds for his readings and where every hue of political opinion has been heard, on the left. When the halls were built in 1841, they could accommodate an astonishing 3,500 people.

Above: the City Halls is a renowned concert venue.

The traditional shoebox-style auditorium is still renowned today, throughout the world, for its incredible acoustics. It's a busy hub for musicians which is well worth checking out: the Glasgow Music Centre inside is a friendly organisation based here which has lots of information about upcoming concerts

Below: Hutchesons' Hall has been at its present location on Ingram Street since 1806.

and public workshops. The BBC Scottish Symphony Orchestra is also based here; in addition, the auditorium hosts performances by the Scottish Chamber Orchestra. For all the latest about City Halls performances and affiliated venues nearby (The Old Fruitmarket, Glasgow Royal Concert Hall) pop in or call 0141-353 8080 or consult www.glasgowconcerthalls.com.

Further down on the left, the pavement outside the City Halls has interesting marblework, created when the street cobbles were renewed and which reflects the area's age.

WILSON STREET

At the junction of Candleriggs and Bell Street, the **Glasgow Police Museum** (www.policemuseum.org.uk; summer Mon–Sat 10am–4.30pm, Sun noon–4.30pm, winter Tue and Sun, same hours; free) gives a historical insight into Britain's first police force as well as exhibits about international policing.

Turning right from Candleriggs into Wilson Street, new apartment buildings blend with the imposing bulk of the old warehouse district and smart design shops nestle below. Con-

Theatre *(see box below)*, a retail complex and smart residential apartments.

Passing the **Brunswick Hotel** on the right, the flats at the corner of Brunswick Street and Ingram Street are a fine example of facade retention. The site was originally the warehouse premises of Campbell, Stewart & McDonald, and was one of the first in the Merchant City to tear out and replace the whole interior while keeping the architecturally important shell. The same thing is now happening with new district council buildings across the road.

HUTCHESONS' HALL

The white building on the opposite side of Ingram Street is **Hutchesons' Hall ❼** (irregular opening times: contact NTS, tel: 0844-493 2134, for the latest hours). Statues of George and Thomas Hutcheson, brothers from a landowning family, peer down from niches in the classical front.

On his death in 1639, Thomas Hutcheson made provision for a hospital for 12 'poore decrippet men'. George added more funds on his death two years later. The hospital was originally in the Trongate, and moved

tinuing right into Brunswick Street, a sandstone Victorian building with huge Ionic columns occupies the entire block. This was the old **Glasgow Sheriff Court ❻**, which opened in 1892 and closed in 1984, having witnessed nearly a century of unmitigated villainy. It once housed a whipping table (now in Strathclyde Police's Black Museum in Pitt Street) and was said to be haunted by a lady in white.

The building is currently being used as the home of the Scottish Youth

Ⓚ Scottish Youth Theatre

Established in 1976, the Scottish Youth Theatre (The Old Sheriff Court, 105 Brunswick Street; tel: 0141-552 3988. www.scottish youththeatre.org) organises an eclectic programme of classes and performances dedicated to young people of all ages, up to 25 years old. Productions are staged in the Brian Cox Studio (named after the Dundonian star of Hollywood blockbusters *Rob Roy*, *Braveheart* and *The Bourne Supremacy*) and theatres around the country.

Above: inside the light-filled Scottish Youth Theatre.

to its present location in 1806 to a design by David Hamilton, with further reconstruction work by John Baird in 1876. The interior is quite simply stunning. It was acquired in 1982 by the National Trust for Scotland (www. nts.org.uk) – whose renovations have been scrupulous and sympathetic. The Trust runs a shop and information room which contains material relating to the Merchant City Trail.

ITALIAN CENTRE AND TRADES HALL

Just past Hutchesons' Hall is the pedestrianised concourse of the **Italian Centre** ❽ in John Street. In this short stretch, on a sunny summer day, Glasgow can consider itself to be a European city. White-aproned waiters rush back and forth to tables of animated diners talking on their

Below: the Italian Centre is a hub of restaurants and cafés that feels like a European city when the sun is shining.

mobiles below the restaurants' canopies. A bronze of Mercury keeps an eye on the shoppers with their Armani and Versace bags, and the view up through the arches of the City Chambers (see p.51) is a symphony in stone. Shona Kinloch's humorous sculpture entitled *Thinking of Bella* and the Zen-calm slow flow of a water feature counterpoise the clamour for *la moda italiana* fripperies.

Leaving the Italian Centre, the squat domed building on the corner of Glassford Street houses a retail outlet. The building was designed by John Burnet and is a splendid example of late Victorian confidence. Slightly further down on the same side is the **Trades Hall** ❾ (tel: 0141-552 2418; Mon– Fri 9am–5pm, Sat 9am–noon; self-guided audio tours available), which is, apart from the Cathedral, the oldest building in the city which still fulfils its original function. It is the home of the 14 trades of Glasgow, which include hammermen, fleshers, bonnetmakers, weavers and barbers (who were the early surgeons). Their symbol – 14 arrows bound together – adorns the magnificent curving staircase which leads into the grand hall. The hall is lined with a magnificent mirrored silk frieze – the 3-D of its time – showing the trades about their business.

The Trades Hall is also the home of the Trades House, whose business these days is mainly philanthropic – it dispenses more than £1 million a year in charity. It is worth a visit, especially for the benches carved by Belgian refugees in the entranceway, the Adam plasterwork and wood ceilings, and the kists, or chests, which are opened only once a year and contain a time capsule of trinkets dating back to 1604.

Return to Glasgow Cross by following Glassford Street south and turning right into Trongate.

Above: the Trades Hall offers a fascinating look at the 14 traditional city trades.

E Eating Out

Café Gandolfi
64 Albion Street; tel: 0141-552 681;
www.cafegandolfi.com; Mon–Sat all
day, Sun lunch and dinner.
A stylish light-filled bar-restaurant
with beautiful wood furniture serving
simply prepared dishes like linguine
with crab, cherry tomatoes, coriander
and chicken. Neighbouring Gandolfi
Fish is its sleeker cousin. £

City Merchant
97–99 Candleriggs; tel: 0141-553
1577; www.citymerchant.co.uk;
Mon–Sat lunch and dinner.
Quality modern Scottish cuisine
specialising in meat and seafood.
Try the superb Loch Etive oysters and
mussels. ££

The Gate and the Secret Garden
62 Trongate; tel: 0141-548 1330;
www.gatetothegarden.com;
daily lunch and dinner.
At the back of this bar there is this
stylish whitewashed space where you
can graze on Eastern-inspired dishes
like king prawn tempura and gin-
ger fried chicken as well as homely
cheesecake and apple pie. £

Ichiban Japanese Noodle Restaurant
50 Queen Street; tel: 0141-204 4200;
www.ichiban.co.uk; Mon–Thur noon–
10pm, Fri–Sat noon–11pm, Sun
1–10pm.
Minimalist, with steaming bowls of
noodles served on long benches. £

Lily's
103 Ingram Street; tel: 0141-552
8788; Mon–Sat lunch only.
This great little café has veggie
options and caters for kids. Alongside
burgers and baked potatoes there
are Eastern tastes including spicy
chilli and vegetable Thai wraps. £

Rab Ha's
83 Hutcheson Street, Merchant City;
tel: 0141-572 0400; www.rabhas.com;
daily dinner only.
This cosy restaurant offers seafood
and meat classics. £

Tron Theatre Restaurant
63 Trongate; tel: 0141-552 8587;
www.tron.co.uk; Sun–Mon lunch only,
Tue–Sat lunch and early dinner.
Serves no-nonsense British dishes
using locally sourced ingredients.
Great pre-theatre meal deals. £

City Centre

This 1-mile (1.6km) tour takes you from the sumptuous George Square and merchants' powerhouses to the shops of Buchanan Street, stopping to visit the Gallery of Modern Art

This half-day walk starts amid the bustle around Queen Street Station and the grand expanse of George Square, which contains the lavish City Chambers and the main tourist information office. Keep your wits about you amid the workaday melee as you will find your eyes are constantly drawn upwards to scan the wealth of mighty stonework built by Glasgow's old governmental and mercantile powerhouses.

Between visits to old bank building conversions and the experience of being swamped by the Buchanan Street shopping crowds, take a breather in the popular Gallery of Modern Art and enjoy the light-filled environs of one of the several swanky Princes Square top-floor eateries.

Highlights

- George Square
- City Chambers
- Glasgow Tourist Office
- Gallery of Modern Art (GoMA)
- Stock Exchange Building
- Buchanan Street and Princes Square Shopping
- Merchants' House

QUEEN STREET STATION AND CITY CHAMBERS

Queen Street Station, the starting point of this tour, runs frequent train services to Edinburgh, Dundee and all points north, as well as a suburban service from the Clyde coast to Lanarkshire. Built on the site of a

witnessed momentous events in the square below, including the raising of the hammer and sickle by the Glasgow Soviet in 1919.

The interiors are a riot of marble, mosaic and alabaster. The vaulted ceiling of the entrance hall alone is covered with one and a half million Venetian mosaic tiles. Linger in the entrance hall, where tours begin and excited Glaswegian school children often linger to admire the Chambers mosaic coat of arms on the floor, with arms that reflect legends about Glasgow's patron saint, St Mungo. There are four emblems: the bird, tree, bell and fish, as remembered in the following verse:

Here's the Bird that never flew
Here's the Tree that never grew
Here's the Bell that never rang
Here's the Fish that never swam

Left: Buchanan Street is always busy with shoppers. **Above:** George Square is a popular meeting place.

quarry in 1842 with a daring curved glass roof, it is Glasgow's oldest station. Beside it, **George Square** ❶ began as a muddy hollow in 1781 and developed into a civic meeting place over two centuries. Its beautiful lawns have been replaced with red tarmac, much to the chagrin of office workers who sunbathed there at the first blink of sunshine.

The **Millennium Hotel** to the right of the station as you face it was, naturally, a railway hotel, and the BR initials can still be seen above the doorway.

The next office block on the left is best sped past in order to come to the **City Chambers** ❷ (Ground Floor only, Mon–Fri 8.30am–5pm; guided tours of whole building, Mon–Fri 10.30am and 2.30pm; free), the towering statement of Glasgow's Victorian confidence, based on the east side of the square. It was opened in 1888 and, according to the architect, was a 'free treatment of the Italian Renaissance'. The ornate front has

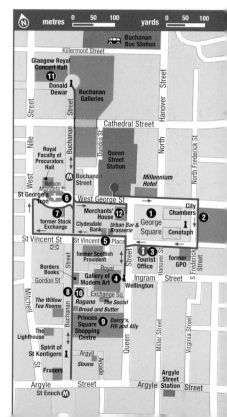

Ⓕ Glasgow Hotel Stories

It was at a Millennium Hotel (see p.51) dinner in 1941 that Roosevelt's World War II envoy Harry Hopkins pledged American support to Britain against Hitler with the biblical reply: 'Whither thou goest, I will go; and where thou lodgest, I will lodge; thy people shall be my people, and thy God my God.' Winston Churchill, who also had a Central Hotel suite during World War II, nearly choked on his cigar. A Glasgow myth goes that Roy Rogers also had a suite in those grand Central Station lodgings, and rode his horse Trigger up and down the main staircase.

Above: the American envoy – and eloquent speaker – Harry Hopkins.

Granite and marble staircases lead like Escher paintings to the council chambers where the Lord Provost (the Scottish equivalent of Mayor) presides over the city's affairs. There are seats for all 79 councillors, all facing the Lord Provost, his Depute, and the Chief Executive, who are seated behind the mace. If you are interested in visiting while the council is in session you can book a place in the public gallery which looks down on the proceedings, or take a pew in the small press gallery, from which much of the lively banter emanates during debate. Civic functions are regularly held in the great Banqueting Hall, under murals painted by 'Glasgow Boys' Henry, Lavery and Roche, which portray the city's colourful history.

GLASGOW TOURIST OFFICE

Passing the white, lion-flanked monolith of the **Cenotaph**, the south side of the square begins with the former General Post Office, which is being redeveloped as luxury flats. Across Hanover Street, the middle office on the block is that of the **Glasgow Tourist Office ❸** (tel: 0141-204 4400; www.seeglasgow. com; May–June and Sept Mon–Sat 9am–7pm, Sun 10am–6pm, July–Aug Mon–Sat 9am–8pm, Sun 10am–6pm, Apr–Oct Mon–Sat 9am–6pm).

It's a grand space for learning all about the city, although queues to gain information can be very long and service can seem a tad slow. If you are

Below: the Cenotaph in front of the City Chambers.

Above: the much-decorated statue of Wellington outside the GoMA.

leaflets and maps though, and to find information about travelling around all of Scotland. A small shop next to the information desk also sells specialist guide books, Ordnance Survey maps for outdoor enthusiasts and an entertaining selection of kitsch souvenirs.

GALLERY OF MODERN ART

Turning left down Queen Street, past bars and fast-food restaurants, the great pillared hall on the right in Royal Exchange Square is the **Gallery of Modern Art** ❹ (GoMA; tel: 0141-229 1996; www.glasgowmuseums.com; Mon–Wed and Sat 10am–5pm, Thur 10am–8pm, Fri and Sun 11am–5pm; free). Guarded by a statue of Wellington by Baron Marocchetti (which revellers grace most Friday and Saturday nights with a traffic cone), the gallery was previously the Stirling Library. It grew out of a house owned by tobacco baron William Cunningham of Lainshaw, and the huge Corinthian columns at the front and the hall at the rear were added later.

really desperate, the tourist office can book accommodation on your behalf but it's not the best service and many leading hotels prefer to deal independently of Visit Scotland, which gives you a clue as to the efficacy of the operation. It's a great place to pick up

Above: a striking view of the roof of the Gallery of Modern Art.

GoMA opened in 1996 to a welter of controversy about its collection. Many critics damned it for populism, but the citizens voted with their feet, and attendance continues to exceed expectations. It is divided into four galleries and there is a great café in the basement by the Martyr's Library. The cavernous ground-floor space retains its columns and original classical features, lending itself to bold pieces like Jim Lambie's eye-popping geometric floor of 2008, entitled *Forever Changes*. The upper galleries use natural light wonderfully, and concentrate on group shows which often tackle challenging themes.

In 2009, the exhibition *shOUT* caused much furore in the right-wing press and even stirred up condemnation from the Vatican. The show focused on gay, lesbian, transgender and intersex life – with explicit images created by the likes of Nan Goldin, David Hockney and Robert Mapplethorpe. One exhibit, *Made in God's Image*, in which visitors were invited to add comments to the pages of a Bible, attracted 600 complaints.

Above: St George's Tron on West George Street.

ST VINCENT PLACE

Returning up Queen Street and turning left, **St Vincent Place** ❺ opens up an august street of banks and offices faced with the full repertoire of the Victorian mason's craft. The Clydesdale Bank on the north side has bas-reliefs, crouching men and encir-

ⓕ Handsome Pubs

Some of Glasgow's gorgeous, solid buildings are now devoted to the Glaswegian passion for having a blether over a drink. **The Counting House** (tel: 0141-225 0160) on the corner of George Square has been converted into a pub and restaurant with splendid interior statuary, cornicing and glass dome above the bar; **The Auctioneers** (tel: 0141-229 5851) in North Court is also a pub and restaurant furbished with the kind of bric-a-brac which used to pass through McTear's showrooms; and **78 St Vincent** (tel: 0141-248 7878) is beautifully lit by the vaulting windows of a former bank, and has an interior reminiscent of Le Chartier restaurant in Paris.

Above: the stunning interior of The Counting House pub.

Above: elegant buildings on St Vincent Place show off the Victorian stonemasonry that characterises much of the architecture in this district.

cled emblems of the towns where the bank has had a presence. Opposite, the former Scottish Provident Building's red sandstone reaches skyward.

ST GEORGE'S TRON AND GLASGOW STOCK EXCHANGE

Passing a variety of city shops on the left, the tour turns right into West Nile Street and right again into West George Street. The church in the centre of the road is **St George's Tron** ❻, built in 1807 to accommodate the westward movement of the city. It was designed by William Stark, who was also responsible for a jail on Glasgow Green and a lunatic asylum. The Tron has a long tradition of being at the evangelical wing of the Church of Scotland: Tom Allan was a key figure in the Scottish evangelical movement of the mid-20th century, and if you pop in today you are sure to be greeted by an enthusiastic minister.

On the north side of the square, Nelson Mandela Place, is the former

Old Athenaeum which, on opening in 1888, offered classes in science, philosophy and literature to more than 1,000 students. It now houses shops and restaurants. Tucked into the corner is the Royal Faculty of Procurators Hall, with the heads of law lords carved on the window arches.

Right: the red sandstone former Scottish Provident Building.

⑤ Pick of the Shops

Che Camille
Floor 6, Argyle Centre, Buchanan
Street; tel: 07862-720 215; Sat–Sun
11am–6pm.
This workshop showcases the talents of young designers, known
as the Glasgow 10. Expect stylish,
weird and wonderful jewellery,
clothes, furniture and lots more.

Tam Shepherd's Trick Shop
33 Queen Street; tel: 0141-221
2310; Mon–Sat 9.30am–5.30pm,
Sun noon–5pm.
Practical jokes, magic tricks, wigs
and masks fill this fun emporium
which inspired Louise Welsh's
novel *The Bullet Trick*.

Tiso
129 Buchanan Street; tel: 0141-248
4877; Mon–Sat 9.30am–5.30pm,
Sun noon–5pm.
With Glasgow being in such close
proximity to Loch Lomond and
the Trossachs (*see p.108*), Tiso is
a useful stopoff for those in search
of outdoor gear – and there's five
floors to trawl through!

Vivienne Westwood
Unit 3, Princes Square; tel: 0141-222
2643; Mon–Sat 9.30am–5.30pm,
Sun noon–5pm.
The British fashion icon brings her
great mix of punk, tartan, bondage and theatricality to the swanky
Princes Square.

The Outdoor Specialist

Above: for all your outdoor needs.

On the other side of the square is
the early French Gothic extravagance
of the former **Glasgow Stock Exchange ❼** building, which recalls the
London Law Courts and is a rare flight
of fancy amid the solidity of its surroundings. It, too, now houses shops.

BUCHANAN STREET

The wide avenue of **Buchanan
Street ❽**, the city's most prestigious
shopping arena, stretches southward.
It starts at Argyle Street, with Frasers
on its domed corner site, and leads up
a Victorian canyon fronted by designer names. In the pedestrianised centre is the winged *Spirit of St Kentigern*
statue, and buskers, from lone evangelists to full string quartets, provide
daily entertainment.

Shopping

Further along on the right is the **Argyll
Arcade**, an enclosed walkway lined
with jewellers' shops, which rightangles back to Argyle Street. Nearby is
the entrance to **Princes Square ❾**,
a beautiful mall packed with trendy
boutiques and bars on several levels.
It is best entered via the central escalator, past the *trompe l'oeil* paintings of
worthies like Sir Thomas Lipton, Keir
Hardie and John Logie Baird.

On the top floor, while looking
down at the mosaic of the central
well, you will not fail to notice the huge
Foucault's Pendulum, a replica of
the device by which Jean-Bernard-Léon Foucault proved the rotation of
the Earth in the dome of the Pantheon
in Paris in 1851. The centre is a shopaholic's dream, with the presence of

**BUCHANAN
STREET**
CITY CENTRE

Above: the ornate Glasgow Stock Exchange building.

top names in fashion such as Vivienne Westwood, as well as upmarket high-street chains like Ted Baker, while the top floor has a range of cafés, bars and restaurants including the stylish Fifi & Ally, Barca Tapas and Cava Bar, Striped Bass and Cranachan.

It's a wonderful building to visit and especially welcome during a rainy spell of Glasgow weather – not uncommon of course – as the twinkly lights, inviting shops and top-floor cafés provide a cheery diversion before braving the elements again.

Galleries and Royal Concert Hall

Back on Buchanan Street, the shopping choice is wide, from chic labels and brands like Hugo Boss, L'Occitane and Apple to the excellent multi-level **Borders Books** bookstore in the old Royal Bank building opposite Gordon Street. Weary shoppers can stop at the Mackintosh **Willow Tea Rooms** (see Eating Out p.97), a replica based

Left and Below: out and about on Buchanan Street.

Above: the Willow Tea Rooms *(see pp.57 & 97)* re-create the designs created by Charles Rennie Mackintosh for a restaurant at the turn of the century.

on the many remnants owned by the City Council, or **Rogano** ⑩, a splendid Art Deco shellfish restaurant situated in the passageway leading to Royal Exchange Square.

Past Graham Tiso, Hobbs and The White Company and back across St Vincent Street to the Stock Exchange,

the view north takes in the **Buchanan Galleries**, an enormous shopping complex development which encompasses several city blocks and a pedestrianised area at the **Glasgow Royal Concert Hall** ⑪ (tel: 0141-353 8000; www.grch.com), the main venue for classical concerts. The centrepiece here is a statue of the late Donald Dewar, credited as the driving force behind the new Scottish Parliament.

MERCHANTS' HOUSE

Returning along West George Street to George Square, the oriel-windowed **Merchants' House** ⑫ (tel: 0141-221 8272; Mon–Thur 9am–12.30pm, subject to functions) reflects the confidence and self-importance of the guilds which created it. Housing the Chamber of Commerce, which is the second-oldest in the world after that of New York, it hosts occasional concerts (see local press for details).

The original Merchants' Hall, constructed around 1600, acted as a

Left: Rogano is an Art Deco *tour de force* and a memorably decadent dining experience.

meeting place for merchants and as an almshouse for merchants and their families who had fallen on hard times. The Hall was rebuilt in the 1650s to a design by Sir William Bruce of Kinross, who would later be architect to King Charles II. The old layout consisted of ground-floor lodgings for old couples and facilities for pensioners. The imposing present-day building was opened in 1877 according to a design by John Burnet; his son added two storeys in 1908. The Merchants' House of Glasgow bought part of the estate of Wester Craigs in 1650, and funded the landscaping of the city's grand Necropolis in the 1830s (see p.22).

Above: the dome of the Merchants' House is topped by a sailing ship.

🄴 Eating Out

Bread and Butter
74 Buchanan Street; tel: 0141-221 4383; http://breadandbutterglasgow. co.uk; daily lunch (Sat until 6pm).
Down a side alley, this café-bar with a club downstairs does great-value British grub including hearty pies. £

Darcy's
The Courtyard, Princes Square; tel: 0141-226 4309; Mon–Sat lunch and dinner, Sun lunch only.
For some café-style panache in the Princes Square shopping centre, book a red-leather booth at this basement joint. As well as decent coffee their varied menu includes Scots Angus burgers and Thai green chilli. ££

Fifi and Ally
Top floor of Princes Square shopping centre; tel: 0141-229 0386; www.fifi andally.com; daily lunch only.
Chic eatery famed for its sophisticated multinational mains, heaped salads, tartines and sensuous sweets including a meringue mountain. £

Rogano
11 Exchange Place; tel: 0141-248 4055; www.roganoglasgow.com; daily lunch and dinner.
Glasgow's homage to the days of ocean liners and cocktails, exuding 1930s glamour. Top-class service and the place for oysters. Dress to impress. £££

Sloans
62 Argyll Arcade, 108 Argyle Street; tel: 0141-221 8886; www.sloans glasgow.com; daily lunch and dinner.
An Edwardian-style pub-restaurant with Grade A listed interiors including a grand ballroom and a cosy, snug bar. Serves simple British cuisine. £

The Social
27 Royal Exchange Square; tel: 0845-166 6016; daily lunch and dinner.
A swanky bar full of suits by day and dressed-up Glaswegians by night with a brasserie menu that includes pasta dishes, juicy steaks and veggie-friendly wraps. There is also a brunch menu at weekends. £

Urban Bar & Brasserie
23–25 St Vincent Place; tel: 0141-248 5636; www.urbanbrasserie.co.uk; daily lunch and dinner.
This stylish bar-restaurant, housed in the former Bank of England HQ, has a monthly brasserie menu with excellent fish and meat creations. Perennial favourite is the fish soup. ££

Tour 5

Going West

This 1¼-mile (2km) walk follows architecturally fascinating St Vincent Street to the historic Mitchell Library, then on to the cutting-edge CCA arts centre – all in half a day

The city has been moving west since medieval times, and, since the more prosperous were the first to decamp, the buildings become noticeably more ornate. Starting the route at the junction of Hope Street and St Vincent Street, the Victorian offices spiral upwards in ever more detailed flights of the stonemason's fancy. Looking south, the clock tower of the Central Hotel looms above Central Station, the main link to the south, in an austere welcome.

UP AND DOWN ST VINCENT STREET

St Vincent Street, named after the naval battle at Cabo de São Vicente, is a thoroughfare devoted to Mammon, so it is fitting that its long incline is

Highlights

- St Vincent Street Free Church of Scotland
- The King's Theatre
- Mitchell Library
- Tenement House
- CCA: Centre for Contemporary Arts

crowned with one of Scotland's finest temples to God. On the way up the hill, there's a beguiling mix of imposing classical, Art Nouveau, Art Deco and modernist buildings including: the old **Phoenix Assurance building** (1913) in American Classical style at No. 78, the eccentric **Hatrack** (1902) with its rich red sandstone,

stained glass and spiky lead roof at No.
142–144, and the elegant 1929-built
Royal **Sun Alliance Building** at No.
200, with its angular Art Deco statue
added in the 1930s.

**St Vincent Street Free Church
of Scotland ❶** is the best remaining
example of the work of Alexander
'Greek' Thomson (1817–75). Thomson, paradoxically, is famous for being
Glasgow's 'forgotten architect', forever in the shadow of Charles Rennie
Mackintosh (see p.92). Like Mackintosh, he wanted to design every detail
of a commission, down to the decorations on the walls. This is the only one
of his three city churches still intact,
and it has been added to the World
Monument Watch for endangered
buildings. Light from enormous windows bathes the sumptuous interior,
and a recently repaired tower, which
recalls India rather than Greece, dominates Blythswood Hill.

On the right, slightly further down
the hill, the needle spire of **St Colum-
ba's Gaelic Church** soars heaven-
wards. It has its roots in the influx of

Left: steep St Vincent Street. **Above**:
Alexander Thomson's St Vincent Street
Free Church of Scotland.

Highlanders who flocked to the city in
the 18th and 19th centuries after the
Clearances, when landlords evicted
crofters to make way for sheep.

The western end of St Vincent
Street is enveloped by the roar of the

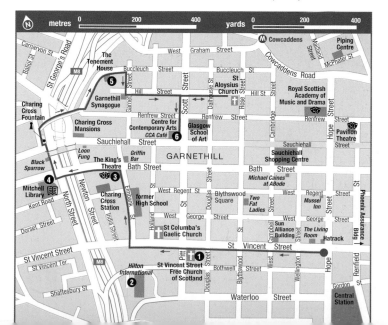

traffic on the M8, which cuts through an underpass on its way to Edinburgh. The marble and mirrored glass tower on the left is the **Hilton International** ❷, a once state-of-the-art hotel (built in 1990) which is looking a bit tired inside and out these days.

TOWARDS
MITCHELL LIBRARY

Turning right into Elmbank Street, the white building on the right is the former **High School**, with statues of Galileo, Cicero, Homer and James Watt. The school dates back to the 15th century, but it has gradually moved west from its original home and is now situated in more space in Anniesland. Today, the buildings are occupied by council offices. On the corner of Elmbank Crescent, the ornate grey-stone building provides the rehearsal rooms for Scottish Opera and Scottish Ballet, two of Scotland's most prestigious companies. It used to be the home of the Institute of Shipbuilders and Engineers, and

a bronze plaque just inside the entrance pays tribute to the engineers who went down at their posts on the *Titanic* in 1912.

The King's Theatre ❸ (tel: 0141-240 1111), on the corner of Elmbank Street and Bath Street, was the most fashionable Glasgow venue of the Edwardian age. Built in 1904, with a lion mascot in stone above the entrance, it provides a stage for a variety of shows, catering for most ages and tastes. Expect lots of West End-style musicals – such as *Chicago* and *Blood Brothers* – stand-up comedy shows from the likes of Frankie Boyle and Dave Gorman, and the odd ballet production or popular musical extravaganza chucked in for good measure. The **Griffin Bar** opposite the theatre dates from the same period. Known as The King's Arms up until 1969, the recently refurbished (2008) Griffin is a 'B' listed building with original wooden interiors, window panels and lead work. It's worth popping your head in and ordering a pint and a sneaky

Below: the Mitchell Library is the largest of its kind in Europe.

Ⓚ Childhood Life in the Auld Tenements

A tour around the 1892-built Tenement House (see p.64) makes for a thought-provoking and fun visit for adults and kids alike. It's not often you can hear the tick-tock of the grandfather clock while poring over old labels and utensils around the basic kitchen range. Eyes and minds wander through the assorted contents – old jam jars, food tins and household bills – and back in time to a much simpler cramped existence.

Above: the Tenement House reveals Glaswegian life in years gone by.

wee dram to take a closer gander at the main bar, with its handsome tiled floor, and back-to-back rows of fixed leather seats.

Mitchell Library

Heading left down Bath Street through a canyon of modern offices, the splendid dome of the **Mitchell Library** ❹ (www.mitchelllibrary.org; Mon–Thur 9am–8pm, Fri–Sat 9am–5pm, closed Sun), adorned with its statue of Minerva, rises above the motorway traffic. It was the legacy of tobacco heir Stephen Mitchell, and, after homes in Ingram Street and Miller Street, the collection moved to the present site in 1911. It is now the biggest public reference library in Europe, and its comprehensive Glasgow Room is a boon and a blessing to those with an interest in the city. Take a peek inside and the friendly janitor will direct you along the handsome marble and dark-wood lined corridors. There's a good little café next to the modern IT suite amid miles of crazy, lurid geometric carpet and books.

The Mitchell Library has fabulous, free resources for those looking to research family history or anyone just curious about the city's past. Level 3 and the Family History Section is manned by helpful and knowledgeable staff who guide people from all over the world in delving into records such as the Glasgow newspaper archive (starting in 1715), censuses, war deaths, parish registers and monumental inscriptions. Leaf though the trade directories to discover intriguing old professionals like the phrenologist – who studied the skull's lumps and bumps to determine personality traits.

Below: the ornate King's Theatre stages a wide range of productions.

Above: the red sandstone grandeur of Charing Cross Mansions.

BACK EAST TO TENEMENT HOUSE

Up North Street past the excellent **Black Sparrow** pub *(see Eating Out, opposite)* and across Sauchiehall Street, the ornate fountain at Charing Cross may not have the cachet of Pisa, but the drunken angle at which it leans is every bit as dramatic. Walking north, head for the pedestrian bridge which spans the motorway. A

Below: the CCA is known for staging an eclectic programme.

pause here affords a close-up look at the graceful red-sandstone curve of Charing Cross Mansions and, on the left, the turrets, arched windows and balconies of St George's Mansions, both testament to the graciousness into which tenement living evolved.

It pays to keep this Edwardian splendour in mind on the walk from the end of the bridge on the path up through grass and trees to **The Tenement House ⑤** (www.nts.org.uk; Mar–Oct daily 1–5pm, last admissions 4.30pm; charge). It lies at the end of the walkway at 145 Buccleuch Street and is fascinating because it offers a glimpse of tenement life. It was the home for 50 years of a spinster who changed nothing in her 'wally close' (tiled common stairway). The gaslit parlour and the black range – and the rosewood piano – are, as the National Trust for Scotland which now runs it says, 'a sure sign of gentility'.

Returning along Buccleuch Street, turn right into Garnet Street and then left into Hill Street: this was for many years the heart of the ethnic Chinese community. On the other side, Italy is recalled by the domed grandeur of **St Aloysius Church**, which is attached to the Jesuit school further up the street.

Above: Charing Cross Mansions detail.

CCA – CENTRE FOR CONTEMPORARY ARTS

Turn left down Scott Street to hit Sauchiehall Street, renowned for its vibrant nightlife, music venues and bars. At No. 350 stands the superb **Centre** for **Contemporary Arts ❻** (CCA; tel: 0141-352 4900; http://cca-glasgow.com; gallery: Tue–Sat 11am–6pm; free), which has six exhibitions a year and mounts an eclectic programme. Alongside the changing visual arts exhibitions there are interactive performance-based art workshops, cinema screenings (lots of independent films, shorts, documentaries and classics) and a superb programme of musical events, ranging from improvised soundscapes to traditional Gaelic nights and dancey DJ sets. Visiting performers and artists from all over the world mean you never know what strange delights might be on the bill. The glass-roofed courtyard café is a wonderful space and their Scott Bar has a stylish terrace with some of Glasgow's best weekend music events.

Ⓔ Eating Out

Black Sparrow
241 North Street; tel: 0141-221 5530; http://theblacksparrow.co.uk; daily noon–9pm.
Stylish bar with decent food menu that includes mains like Red Thai veg curry and Pancetta-wrapped salmon with mustard mash and chive butter. £

CCA Café
30 Sauchiehall Street; tel: 0141-332 7959; Tue–Thur 10am–7.30pm, Fri–Sat 10am–9pm.
Hearty home-made soup, ciabattas, salads and inventive dishes like sautéed king prawn spaghetti, served in a wonderful airy enclosed courtyard. £

Loon Fung
417 Sauchiehall Street; tel: 0141-332 1240; daily lunch and dinner.
Long-established but still admirable Cantonese cuisine, much frequented by the Chinese community. £

Michael Caines at ABode
129 Bath Street; tel: 0141-572 6011; Tue–Sat lunch and dinner.
In the swanky ABode hotel, Michelin-starred chef Michael Caines oversees the sophisticated Scots menu which includes scallops, Mey beef sirloin and Stornoway black pudding. ££

Mussel Inn
157 Hope Street; tel: 0141-572 1405; www.mussel-inn.com; Mon–Sat lunch and dinner, Sun dinner only.
Features the best of west-coast seafood oysters, scallops, prawns and, of course, mussels. ££

The Living Room
150 St Vincent Street; tel: 0141-229 0607; daily lunch and dinner.
Cocktail-style glitz, popular with after-work crowds who tuck into the cosmopolitan menu. Live music is played on the baby grand piano most evenings. ££

Two Fat Ladies
118a Blythswood Street; tel: 0141-847 0088; www.twofatladiesrestaurant.com; daily lunch and dinner.
An elegant dining scene – usually packed – which serves seafood creations including Loch Etive mussels and *linguine alle vongole* (clams) as well as enticing desserts. ££

D.I.Y. Glasgow

Glasgow's music and arts scenes have a D.I.Y. spirit at their heart and, for many, its rough-hewn edge is refreshing over established art centres London, Paris, New York and Venice

The flux of Glasgow's riverside post-industrial landscape – all old decrepit warehouses rubbing alongside sleek, contemporary architecture – seems to flow into the city's creative population. Likewise its indie music labels eschew the corporate and bland, creating a vibrant scene with lots of great bands and venues.

THE GLASGOW
SCHOOL
OF ART
167

AN ART LEGACY

The swinging doors of the Charles Rennie Mackintosh-designed **Glasgow School of Art** (GSA) building continue to whir with the comings and goings of students and artists. It was the home

of the influential *fin-de-siècle* Glasgow Group of modern artists – which included Charles Rennie Mackintosh – and also boasts celebrated alumni such as Alisdair Gray, Ian Hamilton Finlay, and contemporary artists Jim Lambie, Roddy Buchanan and Simon Starling.

Glasgow's D.I.Y. spirit flourished in the late 1970s and early 1980s, when the city was deep in recession and blighted by sectarian violence. New Glasgow Boys and Girls took over warehouse spaces and set up gallery collectives, the most influential being **Transmission** in 1983 (www.trans

continues. The GSA is building a new teaching and research centre. Studio collectives are renovating warehouses and government-led partnerships seek to regenerate the Merchant City by creating a cultural quarter.

A THRIVING MUSIC SCENE

Glasgow's music scene was born from bedroom obsession with exotic sounds. In 1979, the D.I.Y. punk ethos of Postcard Records squeezed Orange Juice and Edwyn Collins from bedroom to Top of the Pops. The city's Gaelic roots, flirtation with Country and popular Americana can be heard in the uplifting Motown beats and West Coast jangly pop of many Glasgow bands. Teenage Fan Club recast the sunshine harmonies of the Byrds and Big Star in late 1980s Glasgow. Some have an art-school sensibility, like Franz Ferdinand, while Electronica DJ duo Slam mined Teutonic beats and Detroit techno music, founding Soma Quality Recordings in 1991.

A good place to start is the independent record shop-café-venue, **Monorail** (www.monocafebar.com), part owned by Pastels front man Stephen McRobbie. It stages film nights, gigs and other cultural events, including the odd appearance of artist David Shrigley.

missiongallery.org). By 1996 contemporary art was part of the mainstream and Glasgow got itself a grand building to showcase its artists: the **Gallery of Modern Art (GoMA)**. Arts hubs **CCA** (Centre for Contemporary Arts), **Tramway** and **Trongate 103** followed.

Both the **Glasgow Art Fair** and **Glasgow International Festival** – the city's answer to the Venice Biennale – attract an international crowd. The impetus

Alongside big venues like the **Scottish Exhibition and Conference Centre** (SECC; see p.10), there are many intimate venues and bars where Glasvegas, The Fratellis and Camera Obscura regularly appear. Top names include the legendary **Barrowland Ballroom** (www.glasgow-barrowland.com/ballroom). **ABC 1 & 2** (www.abcglasgow.com) and **King Tut's Wah Wah Hut** (www.kingtuts.co.uk) host established indie bands. **Nice N' Sleazy** (www.nicensleazy.com) and **Stereo** (www.stereocafebar.com) showcase up-and-coming acts. **Òran Mór** and **Captain's Rest** on the Great Western Road, West End, are also on the music map.

Above: a work by Jim Lambie at GoMA.
Top Left: the band Glasvegas at Nice N' Sleazy. **Centre Left**: a work by David Shrigley. **Left**: the Glasgow School of Art is key to this scene.

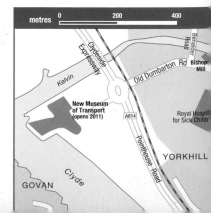

Tour 6

Parks and Galleries

This half-day, 1-mile (1.6km) stroll around the green expanse of Kelvingrove Park leads you to the Kelvingrove Art Gallery and Museum

This walk is a welcome escape from the noisy M8 and is a journey to the heart of Glasgow's Victorian achievements as part of the British Empire. Calm prevails along curving streets lined with handsome Victorian sandstone terraced houses, and the twisting paths around leafy Kelvingrove Park lead to the impressive Kelvingrove Art Gallery and Museum. Nearby is the neoclassical Kelvin Hall and the wonderful Museum of Transport, set to relocate to a futuristic riverside location in 2011.

Highlights

- Lobey Dosser
- Cycling and walking along the Kelvin Walkway
- Kelvingrove Park
- Kelvingrove Art Gallery and Museum
- International Sports Centre and Museum of Transport (until 2011) at Kelvin Hall

Left: an exhibit at Kelvingrove Gallery and Museum. **Above**: the beloved statue of Lobey Dosser.

LOBEY DOSSER AND PARK CIRCUS

Glasgow is peppered with bronze memorials commemorating the cream of Queen Victoria's empire, but the statue which holds the fondest place in the hearts of Glaswegians is of a mustachioed sheriff astride a two-legged horse. It is to be found at the start of this walk on the corner of Woodlands Road, which runs west from Charing Cross and Park Drive.

Lobey Dosser ❶, as the statue is called, was the creation of a newspa-

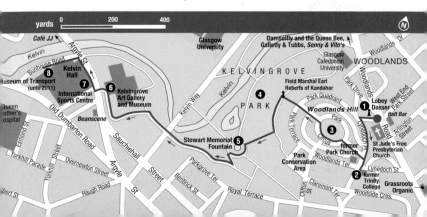

per cartoonist called Bud Neill who, more than anyone before or since, captured the city's sharp but skewed sense of humour. Regulars in the **Halt Bar** across the road were instrumental in raising the public subscription in 1992 to the memory of the Sheriff of Calton Creek and his masked adversary Rank Bajin. The question 'What was the name of Lobey Dosser's horse?' has sparked a thousand pub arguments, and knowing the answer (El Fideldo) will give you instant credibility with Glaswegians.

Leaving the mix of antique shops and restaurants in Woodlands Road, the route runs from the spire of St Jude's Free Presbyterian Church up through the greenery of Woodlands Hill and left into Lynedoch Place. This wide street leads to an area of flats and offices dominated by the Italianate towers of **Trinity College** ❷, formerly the college of the Free Church and now converted into much sought-

Above: a statue of a scholar on a bridge over the River Kelvin.

after flats. Along with the lonely white tower of the Park Parish Church – the rest of it was demolished in the late 1960s – they form a dramatic focus of the city skyline.

Above: autumn colours in Kelvingrove Park.

Ⓖ Cycling and Walking along the Kelvin Walkway

There are lots of fabulous opportunities for cycling and walking in and around Kelvingrove Park and the Botanic Gardens. One less well-known route follows the Kelvin Walkway and links up with the Forth and Clyde Canal towpath at the Kelvin Aqueduct – an impressive feat of 18th-century engineering and architecture, which was once the largest functioning aqueduct in Europe. Ask at the tourist office in George Square for detailed maps and consult the Ordnance Survey Explorer map 342.

Above: a handy marker denotes the Kelvin Walkway.

Turn right into Park Circus Place and enter the splendid oval of **Park Circus** ❸, with its air of Victorian elegance. The grand curving terraces rising to a bluff above the River Kelvin were designed as private housing for the emergent middle classes by Charles Wilson (1810–63) and can justly be regarded as his masterpiece.

KELVINGROVE PARK

They lead to **Kelvingrove Park** ❹, the first custom-built park in the city and the site of three great International Exhibitions, in 1888, 1901 and 1911, which proudly proclaimed Glasgow's contribution to the British Empire.

The Victorians viewed public parks as the lungs of their smoky cities, allowing their workers the physically and morally beneficial effects of clean air and uplifting scenery. **Glasgow Green** (see p.29) was the only public space in the city until 1846, when a grand plan was proposed by the council to create three huge sculpted parklands – **Kelvingrove** in the west, **Alexandra Park** in the east and **Queen's Park** (see p.85) in the south – under the hand of designer Sir Joseph Paxton, of Crystal Palace

fame. The city now boasts more than 70 parks, and, although the recreations reflect Victorian tastes – boating ponds, playgrounds, putting, bowling – the work of the inventive and industrious Parks Department has given each its own character.

Above: a Trinity College tower in the Park district.

The entrance to Kelvingrove Park is guarded by a spectacular statue of Field Marshal Earl Roberts of Kandahar (1832–1914), surrounded by the bas-relief trappings of his Indian campaigns. There is a similar statue of the field marshal in Calcutta. The park itself is a fine example of the ornamental pleasure garden, with winding paths and wide boulevards. Descending into the park, the main thoroughfare and bridge are marked by a memorial to the officers and men of the Highland Light Infantry who fell in the 'South African War' or Boer War (1899–1902). Turning left here, the road leads through dappled shade to the extravagance of the **Stewart Memorial Fountain 5**, a tribute to the Lord Provost who, in 1855, finally managed to secure a supply of pure water to the city from Loch Katrine in the Trossachs.

Turning right past the skateboard park and the duck ponds, the tour

Above: in the Kelvingrove Art Gallery and Museum.

emerges onto the Kelvin Way, and a bridge cornered by four groups of bronzes representing peace and war, commerce and industry, shipping and navigation, and prosperity and progress. They were badly damaged by German bombers in 1941 and restored by sculptor Benno Schotz 10 years later.

KELVINGROVE ART GALLERY

The path opposite the park gate leads to the red-sandstone grandeur of **Kelvingrove Art Gallery and Museum 6** (tel: 0141-276 9599; www.glasgowmuseums.com; Mon–Thur and Sat 10am–5pm, Fri and Sun 11am–5pm; free), a superb repository of one of the finest civic collections in Europe. The gallery had its origins in the paintings of Trades House Deacon Convenor Archibald McLellan, which the city acquired in 1854 along with his gallery in Sauchiehall Street. The need to house these and other displays led to the 1888 Exhibition – a mammoth event attended by Queen Victoria and nearly 6 million of her subjects – and the profits were used as pump-priming money for the new building. The project was conceived on a breathtaking scale, with

Below: an old bus and tram on display at the Museum of Transport (see p.74).

Above: some say that the Gallery was built the 'wrong way round', because the main entrance is from Kelvingrove Park, while most visitors enter from Argyle Street.

its twin towers, which shelter a massive bronze of St Mungo, facing the lacework spire of Glasgow University, and the other side leading down a grand staircase onto sunken gardens. Visited by over 1 million people each year, the Kelvingrove reopened its impressive interior in 2007 after a £27.9 million, three-year refurbishment. Its huge gal-

leries are arranged around two naturally lit halls on either side of the Great Hall which has an immense Lewis pipe organ still used for recitals.

Kelvingrove's Art Collections

The collection, which includes more than 8,000 objects over three floors and many interactive displays, also

Ⓚ Discovery Centres and New Enlightenment

The Kelvingrove Art Gallery and Museum also has much to appeal to children. Glaswegian kids and visitors wander around excitedly and open-jawed, taking in myriad exhibitions, lifelike scale models of animals and the Spitfire LA68 (City of Glasgow Squadron), hanging from the ceiling of the west court. As well as the child-friendly exhibits there are Discovery Centres (info: 0141-276 9505) dedicated to art, environment and history, while the Centre of New Enlightenment (TCoNE; info: 0141-276 9544), in Campbell Hunter Education Wing, offers interactive educational adventures for young people aged 10 to 14 years.

Above: the Spitfire LA68 is suspended above the west court.

Above: the intentionally kitsch figure of Elvis Presley by Sean Read, titled *Return to Sender*, greets visitors coming up the gallery's west stairs.

features many 17th-century Dutch, French Impressionist and post-Impressionist paintings. Rembrandt's *Man in Armour*, Millet's *Going to Work* and Dalí's *Christ of St John of the Cross* are particular favourites. The Glasgow School, in the forefront of the departure from classical tradition, and the Scottish Colourists are well represented, and among the 3,000 oils and 12,500 drawings and prints are works by Rubens, Pissarro, Van Gogh, Degas, Matisse and Monet. Within the walls of this cultural treasure trove, visitors to the West Wing will find a World War II Spitfire hanging from the ceiling *(see box p.73)*.

KELVIN HALL AND MUSEUM OF TRANSPORT

Leaving from the west end of the art gallery, past the 'machine-gun Tommy' war memorial, cross the street to the **Kelvin Hall** (tel: 0141-357 2525), which for many years was Glasgow's foremost exhibition centre, fondly remembered for its formerly-annual carnival and circus, complete with elephants and their distinctive aroma. Built in 1927, it

served for 60 years – including war service as a barrage balloon factory – before its functions were transferred to the Scottish Exhibition and Conference Centre next to the Clyde.

It now serves two functions. The front entrance is to the **International Sports Centre** ❼ (Sun–Tue and Thur–Fri 9am–10.30pm, Wed 10am–10.30pm, last booking 9.30pm, Sat 9am–6.30pm, last booking 5.30pm), which has an international standard running track that can hold 5,000 spectators. Two other halls offer every type of sport.

Round the corner in Bunhouse Road is another entrance, which leads to the **Museum of Transport** ❽ (tel: 0141-287 2720; www.glasgow museums.com; Mon–Thur and Sat 10am–5pm, Fri and Sun 11am–5pm; free), a fascinating collection ranging from motorcycles and fire engines to tramcars, locomotives and steam and motor cars. It has the world's finest assembly of Scottish-built cars, including Albions, Arrol-Johnstons, Beardmores and Argylls. By 2011 the museum is scheduled to relocate to the striking new multi-million-pound Riverside

Above: Kelvin Hall houses both a major sports centre and the renowned Museum of Transport, although the latter is due to move to the Riverside Museum by 2011.

Museum, designed by Zaha Hadid and located on the banks of the Clyde.

The Clyde Room is a tribute to the shipbuilding tradition, with a comprehensive selection of models of warships, ocean liners and merchantmen which were launched into the muddy waters of the river. Many were presentation pieces at the launch – like the *Queen Mary* and the two *Queen Elizabeths* – and the detail and craftsmanship is a joy. The museum also has a truly magical life-sized replica street from 1938, including shops and a cinema, which on a Saturday shows children's films.

Frequent bus services on Dumbarton Road return to the city centre, but first it is worth a quick look down river at the **Bishop's Mill**, with its distinctive wheatsheaf finials. It sits on a natural weir, and the site has been used since the 12th century. It has now been converted for housing.

Ⓔ Eating Out

For the best eating options, see the adjoining Tour 7's Eating Out box, p.83. There's a great café in the Kelvingrove Art Gallery. Other options include these deli-cafés near the beginning and end of the tour:
Beanscene
1365 Argyle Street; tel: 0141-352 9800; daily breakfast, lunch and dinner.
There are three of these outlets in the West End offering a relaxed setting where you can pick from the varied blackboard menu, which usually offers tempting cakes, tapas, nachos, pizza and rice dishes. £

Sonny & Vito's
52 Park Road; tel: 0141-357 0640; daily lunch only.
A popular and friendly deli just off this tour, which serves excellent home-made sandwiches, pies, tarts, salads and sweet treats including huge apricot and chocolate muffins. £
Café JJ
180 Dumbarton Road; tel: 0141-357 1881; daily lunch and dinner.
A homespun place with a hearty menu selection of vegetarian enchiladas, pasta dishes, panini, crêpes and cakes. £

West End

Explore the West End's enthralling academic collections, boho Byres Road and the luxuriant Botanic Gardens on this 1.3-mile (2km) tour, which will take a minimum of 4 hours

In the hungry 1930s, the young bucks of Govan would cross on the Kelvinhaugh Ferry of a Sunday afternoon and stage their own version of the Latin *paseo* (walking out) with the local girls along the bosky grandeur of the Kelvin Way. And to the boys from the shipyard tenements it must have seemed like a foreign country. This wonderful walk takes in the Kelvin Way – which cuts straight through Kelvingrove Park – to the fascinating Hunterian art and museum collections on University Avenue, before exploring the boho shops, cafés and restaurants of Byres Road and Ashton Lane. Our jaunt continues to the exotic hothouses of the Botanic Gardens and ends amid Glasgow artist Alasdair Gray's vibrant murals at the Òran Mór cultural centre.

Highlights

- Kelvin Way
- Wellington Church
- Glasgow University
- Hunterian Museum
- Hunterian Gallery
- Ashton and Cresswell Lanes
- Byres Road
- Botanic Gardens
- Òran Mór

KELVIN WAY AND GLASGOW UNIVERSITY

Starting at the Sauchiehall Street end of the **Kelvin Way**, the Art Galleries open up on the left and the imposing Gothic front of Glasgow University

Left: winter walkers cross a snowy bridge over the River Kelvin.

looms on Gilmorehill. Mature trees canopy the Way after it crosses the bridge with its four dramatic bronzes by Paul R. Montford. On the right is the Kelvingrove bandstand, now sadly derelict (although a restoration is planned), and, by an azalea-studded rockery further along on the left, sit statues of the figures of the great scientist Lord Kelvin (1824–1907) and surgery pioneer Joseph Lister (1827–1912), both in their university robes.

At the end is a cluster of university buildings, with the imposing gothic

Glasgow University Union straight ahead and the Gilmorehill Centre in a former church on the right. Turning left onto the hill of University Avenue is the gilded gatehouse of **Pearce Lodge ❶**, a remnant of the 17th-century Old College in the city centre, which until recently housed the very 21st-century Computing Service.

Up the hill on the right is **Wellington Church ❷**, a grand classical structure influenced by the Madeleine in Paris, with 10 massive fluted pillars supporting its portico. Its predecessor stood in Wellington Street in the centre of the city and attracted a well-to-do congregation, evidenced by the fact

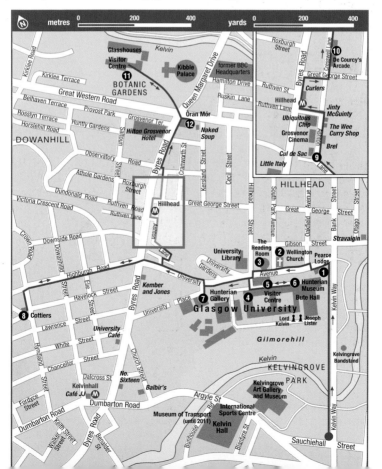

that its war memorial lists mainly officers, with only a scatter of enlisted men. There is a small café in the crypt. Next door is the bright, galleried circle of **The Reading Room** ❸, a quirky but practical study area built in the grounds of Hillhead House, given to the university in 1917 in memory of city merchant Walter MacLellan of Rhu.

Glasgow University ❹, directly across from the Reading Room, is one of the world's great seats of learning, with an outstanding academic history *(see p. 15)* and worldwide influence. The University of Glasgow is the fourth-oldest in Britain after St Andrew's, Oxford and Cambridge. In 1870 it moved to its current site, a leaded-windowed building designed by Sir John Gilbert Scott in what he called 'a 13th or 14th century secular style… with Scottish features'. A complex wrought-iron gate which carries the motto *Via Veritas Vita* contains the names of such

Above: Glasgow University is one of the most prestigious in the country.

luminaries as Bute, Kelvin, Lister, Watt, Stair, Adam Smith and Foulis.

HUNTERIAN MUSEUM

Just inside the gate is a monument to William and John Hunter, the medical brothers whose collection forms the

Above: inside the fascinating Hunterian Museum.

Lord Kelvin's Inventions

The Hunterian Museum's displays dedicated to Lord Kelvin are a big hit with children. There are lots of hands-on activities, scientific instruments, demonstrations and digital images which bring the work of the Victorian scientist to life. Memorable displays include listening to music from a flame, seeing Kelvin's name lit by high-voltage electricity and testing your capacity to be a human battery.

Above: imaginative interactive exhibits at the Hunterian Museum.

basis of the newly refurbished Hunterian Museum, and the award-winning **Visitor Centre** ❺ (Oct–Apr Mon–Sat 9.30am–5pm, May–Sept Mon–Sat 9.30am–6pm, Sun 2–5pm) provides comprehensive information with guided tours of the university (May–Sept Wed–Fri and Sat 11am and 2pm, Oct–Apr Wed 2pm; charge).

A staircase by the Visitor Centre leads to the sunlit quadrangles and the contrastingly gloomy cloisters. Here also is the lusciously ornate Bute Hall and the **Hunterian Museum** ❻ (www.hunterian.gla.ac.uk; Mon–Sat 9.30am–5pm; free), Scotland's oldest, which displays the death mask of founder William Hunter. Its splendid galleries house material of great antiquity, from dinosaurs' eggs and rare material from Captain Cook's voyages to ancient coins and a history of the Romans in Scotland. Leaving by the Visitor Centre and turning left, you reach The Square, which houses the Principal's residence and the University Chapel.

HUNTERIAN GALLERY

Directly across from the university gatehouse is the **Hunterian Gallery** ❼ (Mon–Sat 9.30am–5pm; free) and the Mackintosh House within it (see p.95), with its internationally famous Whistler collection and works by

Rembrandt, Pissarro, Sisley and Rodin. The museum has put together an impressive collection of contemporary art in recent years through the National Collecting Scheme for Scotland. All the recently acquired works have a naturalistic, scientific element which complements the overall collection. The fascinating work of Mark Dion is

Above: there is a rich collection of Old Masters at the Hunterian Gallery.

Above: Mackintosh's *Porlock Weir* at the Hunterian Gallery.

inspired by the powerful historic role of great museum collections such as the Hunterian's. Other contemporary art highlights worth seeking out are Christine Borland's delicate skulls entitled *Family Conversation Piece: Head of Father* (1998), and Matt Collishaw's strutting peacock, which accompanies the works of Whistler.

Above: the Ubiquitous Chip restaurant *(see Eating Out p.83)* is a mainstay of Ashton Lane.

The University Library, which contains more than 2.5 million books and journals, is just a few steps further up Hillhead Street.

BYRES ROAD

Abandoning academia for more hedonistic pleasures, **Byres Road**, at the junction with University Avenue, presents itself as the students' playground. Named after a small *clachan*, or village which once stood there, called Byres of Partick, it is a cosmopolitan mix of restaurants, bars and cafés, and comfortingly solid tenement architecture. Kember and Jones, an upmarket deli and café, and The University Café are both excellent eateries on Byres Road. A brief detour up Highburgh Road opposite the junction leads to **Cottiers** ❽ (tel: 0141-357 3868), a superb theatre, bar and restaurant in a Victorian Gothic church by architect William Leiper, featuring the beautifully restored stained glass and interior design of Daniel Cottier. It hosts shows by Scottish Opera and Scottish Ballet, as well as experimental companies. Jazz is played on Sundays, 5–8pm.

This leads down an alley into an explosion of constantly busy bars and restaurants. In less than 100 yds/m, this narrow, cobbled lane offers Brel (tel: 0141-342 4966), with Belgian beer and 'rustic' food, Cul de Sac (tel: 0141-334 4749), an eclectic bar and restaurant, the Grosvenor Cinema with its huge loft café-bar (tel: 0845-166 6028), Jinty McGuinty's packed Irish bar, the Ubiquitous Chip *(see Eating Out p.83)* and the Ashoka Indian restaurant (tel: 0141-337 1115). Ruthven Lane close by has antiquarian bookstores and vintage and designer clothes.

CRESSWELL LANE

Going north up Byres Road past Hillhead Underground and *Curlers*, an old coaching inn, turn right into Great George Street and then left into **Cresswell Lane** ⑩ for De Courcy's Arcade, a warren of stalls selling linen, jewels, games and records. At the end, turn left and then right again

Above: Ashton Lane is a focus for eating out and nightlife.

ASHTON LANE

To return to the route, just before University Avenue reaches Byres Road, turn right into Ashton Road and right again into **Ashton Lane** ⑨.

Ⓢ Shopping Frenzy

Independent boutiques and foodie outlets line Byres Road while Ruthven Lane and De Courcy's Arcade in Cresswell Lane lure vintage fashion and 20th-century antiques fans. Vintage store **Circa Vintage** (37 Ruthven Lane; tel: 0141-334 6660) bursts with interesting threads, jewellery and curios. At No. 382 Byres Road, **Demijohn** (tel: 0141-337 3600) is a self-styled 'liquid deli' full of whiskies, liquors, oils and vinegars. The sweet-toothed will head for **I Love Candy** (261 Byres Road; tel: 0141-337 3399), filled with tempting old-school sweets, lollipops and Scots fudge. Still on Byres Road, at No. 388, **Boxwood** (tel: 0141-357 6642) features rustic home furnishings, twee treats and quirky clothes. Bookworms will enjoy

a visit to **Voltaire & Rousseau** (12–14 Otago Lane; tel: 0141-339 1811), a wonderfully dusty second-hand bookshop, crammed full of finds and collectable first editions.

Above: there are sweet treats galore at I Love Candy.

Above: inside one the Kibble Palace glasshouses, at the Botanic Gardens.

into Byres Road to the junction with Great Western Road. On the right is the pyramid spire of the former Kelvinside Parish Church, which has been converted into the Òran Mór music centre, restaurant and bar. On the left is the terrace of the **Hilton Grosvenor Hotel**, a quarter-mile repetition of the facades of Venetian palaces. The eastern half was destroyed in a fire in 1978 and rebuilt with glass-reinforced concrete cast from the original pillars.

Directly opposite are the **Botanic Gardens ⑪** (Gardens: daily 7am–dusk, Glasshouses: 10am–4.45pm,

Above: Òran Mór is a cultural centre in a converted church.

winter until 4.15pm, Visitor Centre: 11am–4pm; free), a restful recreation garden relocated from Sauchiehall Street to Kelvinside in 1842, with a herb garden, vegetable garden (highlighting a number of uncommon species) and walks along the Kelvin. The dramatic glasshouses nurture tropical plants. The delicate dome of the Kibble Palace was brought here from the Clyde coast home of John Kibble in 1873. An impressive structure, covering 23,000 sq ft (2,137 sq m), it was originally designed by John Kibble for his home at Coulport on Loch Long in the 1860s, and the components were cast by Walter Macfarlane at his Saracen Foundry in Possilpark.

Prime Ministers Benjamin Disraeli and William Gladstone were both installed as rectors of the University of Glasgow under the curved wrought-iron roof in the 1870s – these were the last public events staged here before the palace became solely used to house temperate plants. After a £7 million restoration, which involved its complete dismantling and the repair of its rusty parts, the palace was reopened in 2006. The ruins of the Botanic Gardens railway station – opened in 1896 and closed in 1939 – can be seen at the side of the gardens through railings.

Just up Queen Margaret Drive on the right is a building that once housed the women students of Queen Margaret College, as well as the old BBC headquarters, which is due to open as a luxury hotel in 2011.

ÒRAN MÓR

Just over from the Botanic Gardens on the city-bound section of the Great Western Road is the fine old Kelvinside Parish Church, converted and opened in 2004 as **Òran Mór** (meaning 'great melody of life' or 'big song'). This cultural centre offers bars, venues and an eclectic programme of musical and theatrical events (including the afternoon A Play, A Pie and A Pint series). Pop

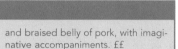

Above: studying the plants in the Botanic Gardens.

in to view the cavernous auditorium and its wonderful murals by artist and novelist Alasdair Gray.

Return to the city centre by bus from Great Western Road or by Underground from Hillhead (Byres Road) or Kelvinbridge (down Great Western Road).

E Eating Out

Balbir's
7 Church Street, West End; tel: 0141-339 7711; www.balbirsrestaurants.co.uk; daily dinner only.
Don't let the soulless interior fool you. This is an excellent choice for a quick curry full of flavour and fresh ingredients. £–££
Little Italy
205 Byres Road; tel: 0141-339 6287; www.littleitalyglasgow.com; daily lunch and dinner.
This popular Italian does takeaways and eat-in pizza, pasta dishes and delicious Portuguese custard tarts. ££
Naked Soup
6 Kersland Street; tel: 0141-334 8999; daily lunch only.
This small wood-panelled eatery is where to find honest, hearty and delicious casseroles, curries and soups including tomato with mascarpone and chickpeas. £
No. Sixteen
16 Byres Road; tel: 0141-339 2544; www.number16.co.uk; daily lunch and dinner.
No. Sixteen serves impressive cuts of fish and meat including sea bream

and braised belly of pork, with imaginative accompaniments. ££
Stravaigin
28 Gibson Street, Hillhead; tel: 0141-334 2665; www.stravaigin.com; Mon–Thur dinner only, Fri–Sun lunch and dinner.
Renowned for using the finest local ingredients in a laid-back ambiance. Standouts include char-grilled Aberdeen Angus steak, grilled monkfish in a broth of mussels, and baked pumpkin, asparagus and sage cannelloni. ££
Ubiquitous Chip
12 Ashton Lane; tel: 0141-334 5007; www.ubiquitouschip.co.uk; daily lunch and dinner.
The Chip is an institution in a converted mews stable. Fresh Scottish ingredients and a wonderful wine list to enjoy amid stylish surroundings and playful artworks by Alasdair Gray. £££
The Wee Curry Shop
23 Ashton Lane; tel: 0141-357 5280; Mon–Sat lunch and dinner, Sun dinner only.
Mother India's chain of curry shops offers a vast array of spicy offerings at reasonable prices. £

Tour 8

South Side

Heading south of the Clyde, this 8-mile, half-day tour takes in parks, grand old houses and arty attractions aplenty, from the Tramway to the Burrell Collection

This tour travels amid abandoned factories and red-bricked chimney stacks, the landmarks of Southside's post-industrial past. First stop is the old Copelawhill Tram Shed reborn as Tramway, a contemporary arts centre renowned for its fabulous visual and performance art shows, and magical Hidden Gardens. Nearby Queen's Park offers magnificent views towards Loch Lomond and Lanark, while heading west, the wide green expanse of the Pollok Estate contains woodland walks, opportunities for mountain biking, and the late 18th-century period grandeur of Pollok House.

The famous Burrell Collection, containing priceless artworks, is displayed in stunning, light-filled galleries close by. There are more uplifting delights at

Highlights

- Tramway
- Queen's Park
- Cycling and mountain biking in Pollok House and Country Park
- Burrell Collection
- Rouken Glen Park
- Greenbank Garden

Rouken Glen and the walled, verdant oasis at Greenbank Garden, with its elegant Georgian mansion built by an 18th-century tobacco merchant. If you don't have the use of a bike, a car would be the best means of transport for this tour, since it is not feasible on foot, and public transport is complicated.

Queen's Park Views

Queen's Park rises to an impressive summit, with panoramic views as far as Ben Lomond in the north and Lanark in the south. Near the main walkway is an oak tree planted by Belgian refugees after World War I and a beech tree planted in 1945 to commemorate the 20th anniversary of the founding of the United Nations.

Left: the sweeping view from Queen's Park over Glasgow and its glorious backdrop of hills.

HEADING SOUTH TO TRAMWAY

Start this walk from Argyle Street at Jamaica Street and, crossing Glasgow Bridge – built in 1899 following a Thomas Telford design – get in the middle lane, pass the classical tenements of **Carlton Place** to the left and head south along Eglinton Street. This area was a riverside hinterland for much of the 20th century and still bears the marks of commerce with warehouses, disused factories and railway arches.

On Albert Drive, the road leading to Pollockshields East railway station, is the fabulous **Tramway** ❶ arts centre (tel: 0141-276 0950; www.tramway.org; Tue–Fri noon–5pm, Sat–Sun noon–6pm; free) below a red-brick chimney stack. It is known for its compelling programme of visual and performance art, dance and experimental music. The Scottish Ballet is now based at Tramway too, in superb new studio facilities.

The majority of the art shows explore challenging, adult-orientated themes which may not be suitable for children. This shouldn't dissuade families from visiting the centre, however, as one of Tramway's most popular attractions is its urban sanctuary, the Hidden Gardens, which sprouted from factory wasteland. Audioguides are available which help you identify birdsong while you are walking around. Tramway's café-bar has views of the garden and is a great place to refuel and relax.

QUEEN'S PARK

Head east via Coplaw Street across to parallel Victoria Road, a wide avenue of small shops, pubs and restaurants which leads to the gates of **Queen's Park** ❷. Although built in the reign of Victoria, and laid out by Sir Joseph Paxton of Crystal Palace fame, these rolling grounds take their name from Mary, Queen of Scots, whose supporters lost the Battle of Langside nearby in 1568. The 148-acre (60-hectare) park

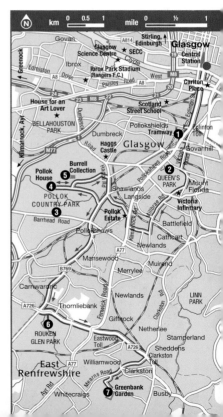

Above: Pollok House mounts an impressive collection of Spanish art, in addition to works by William Blake.

occupies a commanding site, which was considerably enlarged in 1894 by the enclosure of the grounds of Camphill. It is a wonderful place for a picnic and has lots of amenities, should you be feeling more active, including five floodlit tennis courts, pitch and putt, bowling greens and a skateboard park. There is also a pond teeming with birdlife, including tufted ducks, moorhens, mallards, little grebe, coots and mute swans. The large boating pond provides serene moments in the summer months.

TOWARDS POLLOK HOUSE AND COUNTRY PARK

Turning left at the gates, Langside Road, which is not signposted, runs round the park past the **Victoria Infirmary** – a huge hospital serving the whole of the south side of Glasgow – to the monument on Battle Place, designed by Alexander Skirving in 1887, and an imposing stone-cleaned former church which has been converted to the Buddha bar and restaurant.

Going straight ahead at the roundabout, follow Millbrae Road into Langside Drive, turn right at Newlands

Left: a snowy day brings out the sledges in Queen's Park.

Above: light streams into the bucolic Pollok Country Park.

Road (you'll see a sign for Diarsie House School) and follow it to Riverford Road. Go through an area of high-rise flats, past the high chimney stack of the old Pollokshaws 'Steamie', now a sports centre, and onto Pollokshaws Road at the 1897 Town Hall. Turn left here, then immediately right for the entrance to Pollok Estate.

These beautifully sculpted grounds were given to the city as late as 1966 by Mrs Anne Maxwell Macdonald and now form **Pollok Country Park ❸**, where morning joggers and evening strollers enjoy the Highland cattle, heavy horses, art collections and woodland walks. The driveway runs past the Police Dog and Mounted Branch and parkland grazed by 'toffee-wrapper' cattle with their glowering fringes to **Pollok House ❹** (tel: 0844-493 2202; www.glasgowmuseums.com; daily 10am–5pm; charge), a masterful William Adam construction dating from 1752. Its exquisite interior retains many original features and houses a fine collection of Spanish School paintings, and the gardens – including a particularly fine parterre and a full and productive walled garden – are bounded by a lazy curve of White Cart Water.

It has undergone a sympathetic restoration programme, and there is a good café-bar in the kitchen. Pollok Country Park offers wonderful surroundings for cycling and is reached via Routes 7 and 75 of the National Cycle Network (www.sustrans.org.uk), or take your bicycle to Pollokshaws West station from Glasgow Central.

Ⓖ Cycling and Mountain Biking

Pollok Country Park has three mountain-bike circuits suitable for different abilities. **The Green Circuit** offers a gentle ride; **The Blue Circuit** has steeper, more varied terrain and requires more skill; **The Red Circuit** is more akin to wild mountain topography and is not for the fainthearted. Those seeking more two-wheeled thrills should head a few miles further south to **Cathkin Braes Country Park**, venue of the Commonwealth Games 2014 Mountain Biking event.

Above: Pollok Country Park is ideal for cyclists of all levels of ability.

Above: Sir William Burrell's incredible collection of artefacts from all over the world is on display at the famed Burrell Collection.

Above: medieval archways have been incorporated into the Burrell Collection's building.

BURRELL COLLECTION

Retracing the tour and forking left leads to the internationally famous **Burrell Collection** ❺ (tel: 0141-287 2550; Mon–Thur and Sat 10am–5pm, Fri and Sun 11am–5pm; free), the outstanding legacy of the shipping magnate Sir William Burrell, whose collector's instincts and eye for a bargain were on a par with his occasional rival, the American newspaper magnate William Randolph Hearst. He perfected the business method of selling his fleets of ships in a boom period and buying in a slump, and realised his considerable fortune in 1916 when he sold up to concentrate on his first love, art.

The collection is eclectic and idiosyncratic, with more than 9,000 objects from Egypt, Greece, the Middle East and South and East Asia, and tapestries and stained glass from medieval Europe. Favourites with Glasgow visitors are the Degas collection, Rodin's *Thinker* (one of 14 casts made from the original) and the *Warwick Vase*, an 8-ton marble which dominates the courtyard. Volunteer guides with specialist knowledge lead tours of the Burrell Collection – for a detailed list of upcoming tours tel: 0141-287 2550 and consult the website www.glasgow museums.com.

In Glasgow City Council hands
Glasgow city received this fascinating collection in 1944 in a bequest of restrictive conditions, largely concerning Burrell's fears about the potential damage to his treasures from industrial air pollution. This meant that they lay in storage until 1983 when cleaner air and the acquisition of Pollok Estate allowed the construction of an award-winning building with deceptively simple lines, which has drawn as much admiration as the museum's contents.

Medieval archways from the collection are blended with new red sandstone, and some halls have glass walls to the floor, giving the impression that the exhibits are being viewed in the open air. Others are completely enclosed and provide a warmly lit backdrop for some of the world's most exquisite tapestries. The collection also includes exhibits of entire rooms from Burrell's home at Hutton Castle in Berwickshire as well as an excellent café-restaurant.

Above: the imposing *Warwick Vase* is the centrepiece of the Burrell Collection's courtyard.

ROUKEN GLEN PARK

The road out of the park on the left – look out for the carved woodpecker – leads onto Haggs Road. Turn right, get in the middle lane and follow it to Pollokshaws Road and the Round Toll roundabout, then take the B769 for Thornliebank. Stay on this road until the next roundabout

---

ⓚ Family Tours

The Burrell Collection organises special tours for kids and families that explore art, crafts and scientific themes. Perennial favourites include the Weaving Magic tour, which has a hands-on workshop, the Charcoal Fun drawing class with an artist, and Hidden Treasure, which challenges children to solve clues and find the booty, always a popular activity! For the latest events tel: 0141-287 2564.

Above: the collection offers several absorbing child-friendly activities.

Above: a sculptural feature in the Greenbank Garden.

and turn left onto the A727 for East Kilbride. Soon after joining the dual carriageway, turn right into Rouken Glen Park.

Rouken Glen Park ❻ was donated to the city by Mr A. Cameron Corbett (later Lord Rowallan) in 1906 and passed to the adjoining Eastwood Council in 1984, after a dispute over running costs. Its loss to Glasgow was felt on an emotional level by many who remembered school trips to the large boating pond, where a motor launch would carry day-trippers round the islands, much to the indignation of nesting ducks.

Fears of the park's demise, however, were groundless, and a thriving range of commercial concerns – an attractive garden centre, art gallery and a signposted walkabout trail – have given it a new lease of life. The old attractions, however, remain unchanged: the waterfall tumbling into a mossy glen, the walled garden, a golf course and generous parkland.

Below: Rouken Glen's natural waterfall was doubled in height in the early 1800s.

GREENBANK GARDEN

Turning right at the exit, follow the A727 over Eastwood Toll roundabout, through the suburbs of Clarkston to Clarkston Toll, where Greenbank Garden is signposted on the first right after the roundabout.

Greenbank Garden ❼ (garden: daily 9.30am–sunset; shop and tearoom: Nov–Mar Sat–Sun 2–4pm, Apr–Oct daily 11am–5pm; house: Apr–Oct Sun 2–4pm; charge), which lies on Flenders Road, off Mearns Road, is a substantial walled garden which many city dwellers regard as an oasis of calm. It is one of the few substantial properties the National Trust for Scotland has near the city. The gardens surround a tobacco merchant's 18th-century mansion; there are tours of the interior with its remarkable billiard room most Sunday afternoons. A tennis court has been converted into a garden for disabled visitors, with raised beds, and the floral profusion encourages wildlife.

To return to the city, go to Clarkston Toll and follow the signs for the M77, taking junction 3 for the city centre.

Above: the atmospheric walled Greenbank Garden is set around an 18th-century house.

🅔 Eating Out

Boaters Café
Rouken Glen Park; tel: 0141-638 3078; daily, closed evenings.
This homely café located on the edge of Rouken Glen Park is popular with families who queue for the ice cream. Savoury options include panini, salads, pasta dishes and fish and chips. £

The Kitchen Restaurant
Pollok House, Pollok Estate, 2060 Pollokshaws Road; tel: 0141-616 6410; daily lunch only.
Amid the grand basement interiors of this award-winning restaurant, discerning diners are served a limited but excellent choice of mains including beef and mushroom stew. The home-baked cakes are legendary. £

Moyra Jane's
20 Kildrostan Street; tel: 0141-423 5628; Tue–Sat lunch and dinner, Sun–Mon lunch only.
This former bank building has marble-topped tables and wood-panelled walls – suitably solid surroundings for traditional, quality fare including lamb dishes, Thai fishcakes, vegetarian moussaka and massive meringues. £

Tramway Café-Bar
25 Albert Drive; tel: 0141-276 0953; Jan–Oct Tue–Sat 10am–8pm and Sun noon–6pm, Oct–Dec Tue–Sat 10am–6pm and Sun noon–6pm.
An airy space looking onto the Hidden Gardens serving excellent, healthy vegetarian and pasta dishes, superb lamb burgers and sandwiches. £

Mackintosh Tour

Charles Rennie Mackintosh, pioneer of the Modern Movement, left the city of Glasgow a handsome artistic and architectural legacy which never ceases to inspire

Rarely has a whole industry been founded on the designs of one architect, but Charles Rennie Mackintosh (1868–1928) was no ordinary architect. His vision and originality were at the forefront of the Modern Movement, and his imaginative buildings and clean, simple interior design were quite unique. Many of Mackintosh's buildings were neglected until the 1980s, when his importance was realised and restoration commenced. They lie across the city and a comprehensive day tour is difficult, but the following guide highlights the most accessible and representative works, marked with an ⓜ on the maps.

For information on access to Mackintosh properties and about specialist tours contact the **Charles Rennie**

Highlights

- The Lighthouse
- The Willow Tea Rooms
- Glasgow School of Art
- The Mackintosh House
- Queen's Cross Church
- The Hill House
- House for an Art Lover
- Scotland Street School

Mackintosh Society (tel: 0141-946 6600; www.crmsociety.com), or contact the **Glasgow Tourist Information Centre** (see p.123). It's worthwhile buying a one-day Mackintosh Trail Ticket (£12) which allows visitors entry to all participating Mackintosh attractions and unlimited

Left: the House for an Art Lover (p.96) is based on Mackintosh's drawings.

travel on the SPT subway and First bus services. Otherwise during the summer months you can hop on and off the Mackintosh Experience Bus Tour, which was launched with much fanfare and the unveiling of a shocking-pink vehicle in 2009. It is part of the Mackintosh Society's campaign to increase awareness of the architect and its push to have Mackintosh buildings designated as Unesco World Heritage sites.

CITY-CENTRE SIGHTS

Starting in the city centre, **The Lighthouse** (tel: 0141-221 6362 www.thelighthouse.co.uk; Mon, Wed–Sat 10.30am–5pm, Tue 11am–5pm, Sun noon–5pm; charge, Sat free) has a

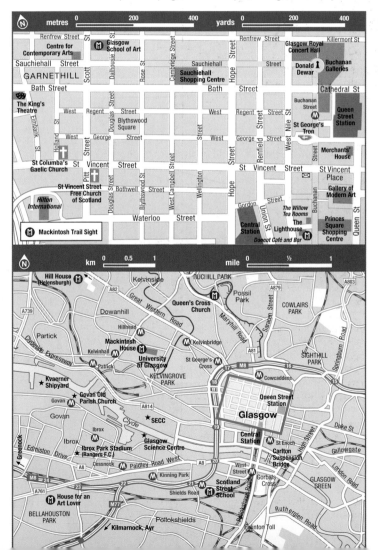

Above: an architectural exhibit at The Lighthouse.

Mackintosh Interpretation Centre to place the artist in his cultural context and to help visitors find his buildings. Built to a Mariscal design beside the tower of the old *Glasgow Herald* building in Mitchell Street, its rooftop platform offers close-up views of his work. It currently hosts a variety of temporary exhibitions exploring design and architectural themes and has a fabulous café. In 2009 the Lighthouse Trust organisation – which was set up to champion Scottish architecture and design – found itself in financial trouble and went into administration. Despite these difficulties, the plan is to keep the building open as a visitor attraction. However, you should check for the latest details before visiting.

GLASGOW SCHOOL OF ART

Along Sauchiehall Street and up Scott Street on the right is Mackintosh's crowning achievement, the **Glasgow School of Art** (www.gsa.ac.uk; guided tours Apr–Sept daily 10am–4pm on the hour, Oct–Mar Mon–Sat 11am and 2pm; charge for tour). One of the most venerable art schools in the UK,

every stone, window and railing is redolent of the architect's unique style.

The east wing was started in 1897 under the influence of revered headmaster Fra Newbery, but the west wing was not completed until 1909. Hefty sandstone block and soaring gridded oriel windows make the first glance of 'the Mac' as you approach from a steep hill laden with drama. Inside there are dark, woody spaces with handsome detailing – the church-like library with

Above: the Queen's Cross Church houses the Mackintosh Society HQ.

Above: the Glasgow School of Art.

MACKINTOSH IN THE WEST END

In 1906, Mackintosh completely re-designed the interior of an ordinary terraced house at 78 Southpark Avenue for himself and his wife Margaret, whom he had married in 1900 just before being made a full partner in Honeyman & Keppie. They lived in it for eight years and, before it was demolished in 1963, the fittings were removed and are now on display as the **Mackintosh House** (charge) in the **Hunterian Gallery** (see p.79; Mon–Sat 9.30am–5pm), which is a brief taxi ride from the School of Art.

Another short taxi hop away from here is the **Queen's Cross Church** in Garscube Road, which is now the headquarters of the **Charles Rennie Mackintosh Society** and is open to visitors. After admiring the red-sandstone exterior with its unusual blocky turrets, dip your head inside to marvel at the interiors. The blue stained-glass window designs play on the Gothic style to startling effect, while the handsome relief carving on wood and stonework complements the feeling of sparseness, light and space. As well as being

like library with its grid-layout wooden pillars and hanging lights is one of the many inspiring spaces Mackintosh created. Studios and windowsills in far-flung corners are bathed in light and provide awesome views. A visit to the building – and better still, going on one of the guided tours with an expert – gives a compelling insight into this working building which continues to inspire art students over 100 years after its inception.

(see p.79; ...)

Ⓕ Rennie Mac's Early Years

One of 13 children of a police superintendent, he was born in Parsons Street, where he would later create the Martyrs' School. He attended night classes in Glasgow's School of Art – then in the McLellan Galleries – before joining Honeyman & Keppie, for whom he did his best work. His first major public building, the former *Glasgow Herald* office – renamed The Lighthouse in a design by Barcelona Olympics maestro Javier Mariscal – was the focal point of Glasgow's year as City of Architecture in 1999.

Above: Glasgow's architectural hero, Charles Rennie Mackintosh.

Above: the House for an Art Lover, set in attractive gardens.

Back to School

Kids and adults will enjoy a look around Scotland Street School's three classroom reconstructions, which show the changing face of teaching and childhood from the Victorian era through World War II to the classroom of the 1950s and 1960s. Particularly evocative are the barrel-vaulted cookery room, cloakrooms, and ceramic-tiled drill hall which have been restored to Mackintosh's original 1906 designs.

Above: an old classroom reconstruction at Scotland Street School.

the best place for finding out about Mackintosh events and tours, the Mackintosh Church at Queen's Cross has a superb library. The shop stocks an extensive range of Mackintosh books and objects based on the great man's designs.

THE HILL HOUSE AT HELENSBURGH

The Hill House (tel: 01436-673 900; Apr–Oct 1.30–5.30pm; charge) is not in Glasgow, but it should be included in any tour of Mackintosh works. A 40-minute train ride away in Helensburgh (First Scotrail; tel: 08457-484 950), it is by far the most attractive of his domestic commissions. Built on a commanding site for the publisher Walter Blackie, the fittings have been meticulously conserved by the National Trust for Scotland.

SOUTHSIDE MASTERPIECES

House for an Art Lover (www. houseforanartlover.co.uk; Apr–Sept Mon–Wed 10am–4pm, Thur–Sun 10am–1pm, Oct–Mar Sat–Sun 10am–1pm; tel: 0141-353 4770; charge) was created from a portfolio which Mackintosh presented for a design competition in 1901. Following his drawings, the house was built in a beautiful parkland setting beside the Victorian walled garden in Bellahouston Park, and contains striking details and interiors as well as a café and shop. The nearest Underground station is Ibrox; mainline station, Dumbreck. The house is about 15 minutes by taxi from the city centre.

Scotland Street School (tel: 0141-287 0500; www.glasgowmuseums.com; Mon–Thur and Sat 10am–5pm, Fri and Sun 11am–5pm; free) is most easily reached by Underground at Shields Road station, from whose entrance the twin towers of leaded glass and red sandstone stand out from across the road.

Built between 1903 and 1906, the school is clearly Glasgow-style and offers a fascinating look at developments in Scottish education. There are interactive displays which explore the school world and design tools to see if you can match the master draughtsman Mackintosh. Even more fascinating are the accounts of former pupils' recollections of their school days. The archive follows the decades, detailing the minutiae of childhood and back-

Above: inside the elegant House for an Art Lover.

ground events in Scots and world history. Themes covered include classroom discipline, school trips, school attire, evacuation and World War II, playground antics and the changing local environment. Their excellent Back to School role-playing programme has interactive displays that allow the visitor to experience the classes of yesteryear *(see box opposite)*.

Ⓔ Eating Out

The Doocot Café and Bar
The Lighthouse, 11 Mitchell Lane; tel: 0141-221 1821; www.doocot.co.uk; daily lunch only.
On the top floor of The Lighthouse, Scotland's centre of design and architecture, the Doocot Café and Bar is housed in the Mackintosh-designed former home of the *Herald* newspaper. Expect stylishly presented and simply prepared pasta, seafood, veggie and meat dishes. The classic Charles and Ray Eames chairs and tables here are mid-20th-century heirs of the modernist aesthetic Mackintosh helped shape. £

The Willow Tea Rooms
97 Buchanan Street; tel: 0141-204 5242; www.willowtearooms.co.uk; Mon–Sat 9am–5pm, Sun 11am–5pm. This is a faithful re-creation of the innovative design work Mackintosh carried out for well-known restaurateur Kate Cranston at the turn of the 20th century. The originals of the White Room and the Blue Room are in the care of Glasgow City Council. More Mackintosh interiors, afternoon tea and scones can be enjoyed at the other Willow Tea Rooms located at 217 Sauchiehall Street (tel: 0141-332 0521).

Excursion to Burns Country

On the trail of poet Robert Burns, visiting auld hair and Rabbie-raising haunts – including the Bachelors' Club and Burns Cottage, his birthplace

For a' that, an' a' that,
It's coming yet for a' that,
That Man to Man, the world o'er,
Shall brothers be for a' that

Scots, with their long tradition of struggle for social justice, are particularly partial to the egalitarian theme that runs through the works of the Ploughman Poet, their National Bard, Robert 'Rabbie' Burns (1759–96). The memory of his turbulent life – replete with love, laughter, triumph and despair – is kept alive at Burns Suppers across the world at the end of January, and the minutiae of his dalliances, though a source of fascination for Scots, are fully chronicled elsewhere.

Burns's associations with Glasgow were tenuous – some minor dealings with publishers – but the literary legacy he left and the memorials to his origins in the Burns Country are easily accessible from the city and make a fascinating day out. A car is required for this excursion that takes you down to the southwest coast taking in the

Highlights

- Burns House, Mauchline
- Highland Mary Monument
- Bachelors' Club
- Ayr
- Burns Cottage
- Auld Alloway Kirk
- Brig O'Doon
- Burns National Heritage Park
- Souter Johnnie's Cottage

Leaving the village on the B743, the road winds towards **Failford** ②, a scatter of houses in a small dip. A grassy path behind a sign to Failford Gorge – particularly easy to miss – leads to a monument to **Highland Mary**, the mysterious but beautiful woman for whom Burns wrote *My Highland Lassie O* and from whom he took his last farewell here in 1786. This is one of the lesser Burns monuments, but the simplicity of it is in stark contrast to the Heritage Park at Alloway, and the inscription on the pillar is touching:

> *That sacred hour can I forget,*
> *Can I forget the hallowed grove,*
> *Where by the winding Ayr we met,*
> *To live one day of parting love.*

Left: Crossraguel Abbey, dusted with snow. **Above**: Burns' old hangout, the Bachelors' Club.

BACHELORS' CLUB

Past Failford, a brief diversion on the right leads to Tarbolton, a farming

various Burns-related monuments and sights, including the new Robert Burns Birthplace Museum at Alloway.

MAUCHLINE AND FAILFORD

Leave the city on the M8 westbound and join the M77, then the A77 heading for Ayr. Turn off just past Kilmarnock at the A76 signposted for Dumfries. This road leads through typical Ayrshire countryside – rich farmland with copses of wind-beaten trees and straggling streams – to the village of Mauchline, on the outskirts of which stands the red-sandstone Scots baronial folly of the **National Burns Memorial Tower**, established in 1896, and worth a look. The **Burns House** ① (tel: 01290-550 045; early May–late Sept Tue–Sun 10am–5pm, Easter–Oct Tue–Sun 10am–5pm; free) in which the poet lived is in the village centre, as is **Poosie Nansie's Tavern**, where he was known to take his pleasure. This ale house is said to have inspired part of his cantata *The Jolly Beggars*.

Above: the spooky graveyard at Auld Alloway Kirk.

community where the National Trust for Scotland is the custodian of the **Bachelors' Club ③** (tel: 01292-541 940; 1 Apr–30 Sept Fri–Tue 1–5pm, last admission 4.30pm; morning visits available for pre-booked groups; charge). It is a 17th-century thatched house just off the main road through the village, where the poet and his cronies formed a debating club with, it has to be said, easy access to the inn next door. It was almost certainly here that Burns was introduced to the Freemasonry which shaped his philosophy of the brotherhood of Man.

FROM AYR TO THE NEW BURNS MUSEUM

Returning to the B743, it is 6 miles (10km) to **Ayr ④**, a bustling resort town with beautiful sandy beaches, excellent shops and a classical statue of Burns in the main square. Crossing the main road over the River Ayr, the 15th-century pedestrian bridge on the left is the **Auld Brig**, the harbour is on the right and the imposing 126ft (38m) pillared steeple straight

ahead is Ayr Town Hall. Burns was baptised in the Auld Kirk.

Heading out of town on the A719 signposted for Maidens, look for a sign for the Heads of Ayr, then turn left at the first sign for **Alloway**, a pretty village of rose-entwined cottages which is at the heart of the Burns Country. A

Below: the 'Auld Brig o' Doon'.

Ⓖ Burns by Bike

During the summer months Cycle Ayrshire (tel: 01290-550 276; www.cycleayrshire.co.uk) organises various Burns by Bike cycle outings led by expert riders over mainly minor roads. There is a variety of excursions, catering for all abilities including beginners and families. The more taxing 38-mile (60km) ride starts at Rozelle Park in Ayr, then takes in Tarbolton Mauchline, Coylton and Dalrymple before returning to Ayr. A decent level of fitness is suggested for this ride. For the latest programme see the website and phone details above.

built with his own hands and where he instilled young Robert's love of language and learning. The new museum contains the most important collection of the poet's work, including the original copy of the *Kilmarnock Edition*, the first collection of poems which he published to raise cash in order to emigrate to Jamaica. Visitors are occasionally greeted by a cheerful young man in a frock coat who ushers you towards the state-of-the-art technology, which aims to bring the life, loves and demons of the poet to life. The nearby **Tam O'Shanter Experience** (Apr–Sept 10am–5.30pm, Oct–Mar 10am–5pm; free) – a visitor centre named after his most famous poem, a tale of warlocks and witches which warns of the dangers of one dram too many – is due to close in the autumn of 2010.

handy car park on the left at the junction with the B7024 to Maybole serves the **Burns Cottage** ❺ (Apr–Sept daily 10am–5.30pm, Oct–Mar daily 10am–5pm; charge), the birthplace of Burns, and the **Robert Burns Birthplace Museum**, due to open in 2010. His birthplace is a clay-wall-and-thatch house, which the poet's father William

AULD ALLOWAY KIRK

Auld Alloway Kirk ❻, just a little further on, is a 16th-century refuge which was a ruin even in Burns's day and was last used in 1756. Its gloomy graveyard holds the remains of Burns's father, and the mossy crypts and worn

Below: Burns Cottage, the birthplace of the beloved Scottish bard.

Above: the 13th-century Brig O'Doon features in Burns's poetry.

stones with their goblin carvings are a suitably chilling setting for the dance of the witches as the Devil – '*a tousie tyke, black, grim and large*' – played the pipes and '*gart them skirl*'. Those of a nervous disposition should ensure their visit ends before nightfall.

When Tam, inspired by John Barleycorn, interrupted their dance with the shout: '*Weel done, Cutty Sark*', his mare Meg fled to **Brig O'Doon** nearby to escape minus '*her ain grey tail*'. This 13th-century cobbled bridge with its ancient arch now stands below the **Burns Monument**, a Grecian tower designed by Thomas Hamilton and opened in 1823 at the then-huge cost of £2,085. It is surrounded by a garden of heathers and rose bowers which leads to the car park of the **Burns National Heritage Park** ❼ (tel: 01292-443 700; www.burns heritagepark.com; charge).

The B7024 carries on to **Maybole**, where Burns's father and mother met in 1756. Joining the A77, signposted for Stranraer, the road leads past the dramatic 13th-century ruins of **Crossraguel Abbey** ❽ with its abbot's

tower and dovecote, to the village of Kirkoswald. Here the National Trust for Scotland maintains the thatched **Souter Johnnie's Cottage** (tel: 01655-760 603; Apr–Sept Fri–Tue 11.30am–5pm; charge), a representation of the daily life of the cobbler who was the inspiration behind Tam O'Shanter's '*ancient, trusty, drouthy crony*'.

This is a long but fascinating run which could be well rounded off with refreshment in the excellent **Westin Turnberry Resort Hotel** (tel: 01655-331 000), just a few miles further south, and scene of memorable moments in Open golf history.

🄴 Eating Out

Ayr
Fouters Bistro
2a Academy Street; tel: 01292-261 391; www.fouters.co.uk; Tue–Sat lunch and dinner.
Down in the vaults of an old bank, this renowned place serves excellent Scots fare using quality ingredients such as Gressingham duck, Ayrshire lamb and John Dory. ££

Tour 11

Excursion to Loch Lomond

An 80-mile (130km) foray into the Highlands, Loch Lomond and The Trossachs National Park, dipping into Britain's largest lake and visiting beguiling villages

You tak' the High Road,
and I'll tak' the Low Road,
and I'll be in Scotland afore ye.

The words of the Loch Lomond song distil the romance of the glens for Scots the world over, but for the most part, the reality of the High Road these days is a wide dual carriageway. Following signs for Crianlarich, the A82 continues westwards from Great Western Road in the centre of Glasgow through the western suburbs along the north bank of the Clyde past Bowling, Dumbarton – the ancient capital of Strathclyde, with its castle on the rock – and Balloch.

This is a long excursion, but once at the loch, the roads mellow out and the

Above: peaceful Loch Lomond.

Highlights

- Balloch
- Drymen
- Balmaha
- Priory of Inchmahome
- Aberfoyle
- Loch Katrine

countryside ranges from the lush and rolling to true Highland drama. The route includes points at which you have to double back on yourself, but generally not for more than a few miles.

LUSS, ON THE BANKS OF LOCH LOMOND

The first is at Loch Lomond itself. Still following the Crianlarich signs,

Above: Balloch's visitor centre incorporates a fascinating aquarium.

head first for the village of **Luss** ❶. Although surrounded on the outskirts by tourist services, the rose-clad cottages and the old pier are attractive. On the other side of the main carriageway, a farm road signposted for Glen Luss runs up to some of the best hill-walking within easy reach of the city. A series

Below: picturesque cottages in Luss.

of Corbetts (Scottish hills between 2,500ft/76m) and the 3,000ft (914m) Munros affords spectacular views to the Clyde estuary and the western islands. The weather in the mountains can change quickly, so always carry a map, and dress warmly (see p.109).

BALLOCH, DRYMEN AND BALMAHA

Returning south, turn left at the roundabout signed for **Balloch** ❷ and left again at the next roundabout. This leads into the heart of Loch Lomond's only town of any size. It hosts **Loch Lomond Shores** (tel: 01389-722 406; www.lochlomondshores.com; charge), a modern visitor centre with shops, café and innovative aquarium (tel: 01389-721 500; charge) complete with sharks, which is the centrepiece of the newly created National Park, Scotland's first. Boats of all shapes and sizes crowd the banks and pontoons as the loch empties into the River Leven on its way to the Clyde.

The A811, signposted for Drymen, wanders through undulating farmland, passing only one village of note, **Gartocharn** ❸, with its atmospheric pub, **The Hungry Monk** (tel: 01389-830

448; daily 11am–midnight). The small hill at the back is called **Duncryne** and is worth the gentle effort of the climb for views across the water-meadows of the southern loch, the wooded islands and the ever higher hills in the distance, including Ben Lomond.

At the junction with the A809, turn left to **Drymen ❹**, a delightful village, lying 11 miles (18km) north of Glasgow. It retains a charming rural atmosphere, with the main road winding past the Church of Scotland cemetery and the **Buchanan Arms Hotel** (tel: 01360-660 588) to a village square. The cosy **Clachan Inn** (tel: 01360-660 824), established in 1734, and on the corner of the square, is a good place to eat or to enjoy a wee dram.

The B837 from the centre runs 5 picturesque miles (8km) to **Balmaha ❺**, a village lying on the Highland Boundary Fault, a geological line separating the Highlands from the Lowlands. A scatter of white-washed houses surrounds the small inlet where **Balmaha's boatyard** (tel: 01360-870 214) caters for fishermen and loch cruisers, and offers places on the regular mailboat round the islands – an unusual day trip. The pleasant **Oak Tree Inn** (tel: 01360-870 357) is a good accommodation option or place to enjoy hearty pub food and real ale. A path leads from the main car park to the Conic Hill, the dramatic rise behind the village from which it is possible to see that the 37 islands in the loch are part of the same geological formation.

LAKE OF MENTEITH

Returning to Drymen, the A811 meanders north and east before joining the A81 north across the flatlands towards the hills of the Queen Elizabeth Forest. At the Rob Roy Motel, the route goes left to Aberfoyle, but turning right along the A81 for a short

Ⓖ West Highland Way

The West Highland Way, a 95-mile (152km) walk from Milngavie, on the outskirts of Glasgow, to Fort William, starts at a granite obelisk in Douglas Street. The route follows ancient and historic communication tracks as well as drove roads, military roads and disused railway tracks. The first 5-mile (8km) stage to Carbeth involves 500ft (148m) of ascent – a tame but enjoyable preamble to later challenges like climbing the Devil's Staircase below Glencoe's jagged Aonach Eagach ridge. See also www.west-highland-way.co.uk.

Above: the beautifully scenic terrain.

Above: Balmaha's boatyard is the place to pick up a loch cruiser.

distance to the B8034 brings you to the island priory of **Inchmahome** ❻ (Apr–Sept daily 9.30am–4.30am; charge includes ferry) on the Lake of Menteith, the only 'lake' in Scotland. These beautiful 12th-century

Below: the historic Inchmahome priory, on the Lake of Menteith.

Augustinian remains once sheltered Mary, Queen of Scots. The **Lake of Menteith Hotel** (tel: 01877-385 258) combines fine cuisine with memorable views over the lake.

ABERFOYLE

Follow the A821 for the Trossachs. You'll next hit **Aberfoyle** ❼, a market village and tourist honeypot, with a variety of pubs and restaurants.

The road north negotiates a startling series of hairpin bends as it climbs past the **David Marshall Lodge** to the Duke's Pass – watch out for a kilted piper here in the summer – then descends to Loch Achray. One of the small peaks on the far side of the loch is **Ben A'an** which, like Duncryne, more than richly rewards the effort of conquering it. It affords an unparalleled vista of Loch Katrine, which has changed only in minor detail since Sir Walter Scott was inspired by the scenery to write *The Lady of The Lake* (1810).

Before Ben A'an, the main road branches off to **Loch Katrine** ❽, where the steam yacht *Sir Walter*

Scott sails on Glasgow's water supply (Apr–Oct; always call to check times; tel: 01877-332 000/376 316). Bicycles are also available to hire for a recommended ride along the lovely lochside road.

For the quickest journey back to Glasgow, travel the 10 miles (16km) to Callander, then on to Stirling to join the M9.

Above: the banks of Loch Katrine are ideal for a peaceful bicycle ride.

E Eating Out

Balloch

Balloch House Vintage Inn
Balloch Road; tel: 01389-752 579; daily lunch and dinner.
Serves hearty pub meals like fish and chips and seafood alongside more adventurous dishes. £

Near Balloch

Cameron House Hotel
A82; tel: 01389-755 565; www.devere. co.uk; Cameron Grill: daily breakfast and dinner; Martin Wishart's: Wed–Fri dinner, Sat–Sun lunch and dinner.
This stylish, luxurious lochside former stately home offers several dining options. Our recommenda-

tions are the Cameron Grill – great for bountiful breakfasts and juicy Angus steaks – and Martin Wishart's sophisticated eatery, which serves delicious dishes such as langoustine ravioli and turbot with sweet garlic cannelloni. £–£££

Duck Bay Marina
tel: 01389-751 234; www.duckbay. co.uk; daily lunch and dinner.
This modern hotel restaurant has large picture windows providing glorious views of Loch Lomond. Expect a varied menu which offers traditional Scots seafood classics like Cullen Skink alongside pasta dishes and crêpes. ££

Loch Lomond

Everyone has heard of it, but the Loch bit of Loch Lomond is just one of the shimmering jewels in what is Scotland's most famous and diversified National Park

OUTDOOR TREATS

Loch Lomond and the Trossachs National Park stretches a little west of the Loch, north to Tyndrum, east to Callander and south to Balloch. Straddling the West Highland fault line, the heather-clad hills abound with 'darksome glens and gleaming lochs', as wrote Scottish legendary author Sir Walter Scott.

This area has a magnetism for walkers, cyclists and those who love water sports. Loch Lomond and the Trossachs National Park Gateway Centre in Balloch (www.loch lomond-trossachs.org) has every kind

of information about the park, including geological history, walking routes, cycle paths and details about all the guides and companies who provide tours, mountain-bike excursions, horse riding, fishing and boat trips on the lochs (notably the *Sir Walter Scott* steamer on Loch Katrine; *see p.106*).

WALKING COUNTRY

There is a multitude of easy and short walks, such as the **Creag an Tuirc** walk, which begins at Balquidder (2.5miles/4km, about 2hours), and the hillier **Cruach Tairbeirt** walk (4.7miles/ 7.5km, about 3

Flora and Fauna

As you travel away from the sparkling shores of the loch, spectacular hills, glens with densely wooded forests and a real sense that you are surrounded by the wild awaits you. The National Park boasts 200 species of birds, from buzzards and, in remoter areas, ospreys and golden eagles, to peregrine falcons, pied flycatchers and capercaillies – although you are more likely to hear the cricking noise of these than see them amongst the heathery thickets. Home to 25 percent of Britain's wild plant species, there are 500 flowering species and ferns, with rarities such as the wood anemone, wood sorrel and, magnificent in May, the thickest blankets of bluebells. And as for fauna, take your time and keep quiet and you have some chance of being in the presence of – if not seeing – red deer, polecats, pine martens and wildcats. Meanwhile, Loch Lomond is the largest freshwater loch in the UK; within it swim fish, salmon, pike and, only found in one other place, powan – a whitefish.

hours), taking you up to 1485ft (450m). In exchange for your efforts you receive glorious views of Loch Lomond – weather permitting.

If you must climb a hill, try the **Ben Ledi**, classified as a Corbett, a smaller set of Scottish hills (5miles/8km, about 4 hours). It might be wee but on a clear day you can see the Firth of Forth from the summit at 2,508ft (760m). For those craving to bag a Munro, Scotland's

highest peaks, 3,465ft (1,050m) -high **Ben Lui** (13miles/21km, about 7 hours) is a must-climb. For much of the year its Coire Gaothaich (Windy Corrie) is filled with snow, lending it an alpine character. Ben Lui is reached from Tyndrum.

For those with time, the inclination and broken-in boots, the famous **West Highland Way** (92½ miles/148km, up to 2,650ft/800m), from Milngavie to Fort William is one of the most trampled and loved walks of Scotland. It will take between 7 and 10 days.

Whatever walk you choose to do, be prepared for a dramatic change in the weather, even in the warmest months, and have proper footwear, a map and compass (the ability to use these properly is a must too!) as well as waterproof clothing. Also, leave word of your plans with your accommodation.

Above: the Loch Lomond park is perfect walking country. **Top Left**: a Loch Lomond walkway. **Centre Left**: a local pine marten. **Bottom Left**: the rare, vocally impressive capercaillie, a woodland grouse.

Tour 12

Excursion to Clyde Valley

Two country parks, riverside walks, the David Livingstone Centre, Craignethan Castle and fascinating New Lanark make this a stimulating jaunt

Highlights

- Strathclyde Country Park
- Duke of Hamilton's Mausoleum
- David Livingstone Centre
- Chatelherault Country Park
- Craignethan Castle
- Lanark
- New Lanark

The River Clyde, the wonderful Clyde,
The name of it thrills me and fills me
with pride.

When Glaswegians sing praise of the river that gave their city meaning, they think of the clatter of shipyards and the sway of giant cranes. But further down the valley is an altogether different river, wandering through gentle hills and watering fertile orchards and fruit farms. This 45-mile (70km) tour requires a car, or a bike for the very fit, taking in country parks, lots of intriguing history and a Unesco World Heritage Site at New Lanark.

STRATHCLYDE COUNTRY PARK

The M8 snakes through the centre of Glasgow, and it is possible to join it at many points. Once on the eastbound carriageway, follow signs for Carlisle and Edinburgh through the industrial eastern suburbs until you reach junction 8 with the M73, then follow signs for Carlisle.

Off the A723 between a cluster of Glasgow's satellite towns – including **Hamilton and Motherwell** – is

✂

Left: the picturesque Falls of Clyde.
Above: there are thrills of all sorts at Strathclyde Country Park.

Strathclyde Country Park ❶. It's accessible via junction 5 of the M74. This huge recreation area includes a man-made loch that offers sailing, windsurfing and water-skiing, and also an amusement park, **M&D's** (tel: 01698-333 777; www.scotlands themepark.com) with some of the biggest rides in Scotland.

The **Low Parks Museum** (tel: 01698-328 232; Mon–Sat 10am–5pm, Sun noon–5pm; free), built on the site of the Hamilton Palace, complete with new mezzanine café, is located on Muir Street. It tells the turbulent history of the town, its regiment – the Cameronians – and the Hamilton family, whose spectacular **Mausoleum ❷**, built by the 10th Duke in the 1840s, has impassive stone lions guarding the enormous bronze doors and beautiful marblework within.

DAVID LIVINGSTONE CENTRE

A few miles up the A724 at Blantyre is the **David Livingstone Centre ❸**

(www.nts.org.uk; Apr–Dec Mon–Sat 10am–5pm, Sun 12.30pm–5pm; charge), a memorial to Scotland's greatest missionary explorer, who was born here in 1813. Growing up as a poor factory boy, he led an eventful life which included the discovery of the Victoria Falls on the border between Zambia and Zimbabwe while on a journey across the African continent in 1855. He died of dysentery in 1873 while searching for the then unknown source of the Nile.

CHATELHERAULT COUNTRY PARK

Returning through Hamilton, join the A72 for Lanark and, as the suburbs give way to countryside, the gates of **Chatelherault Country Park ❹** (Apr–Sept Mon–Sat 10am–5pm, Sun noon–5.30pm, Oct–Mar Mon–Sat 10am–5pm, Sun noon–5pm) open up on the right. A Visitor Centre, once the kennels for the hunting dogs of the Duke of Hamilton, butts onto the main building, designed by William Adam for the Fifth Duke and completed in 1744. The building fell into dereliction – mining subsidence has added a jaunty slope to some floors – and a masterful restoration was completed in 1987 allowing full appreciation of the superb plasterwork showing ornate figures from classical mythology.

Above: the fascinating New Lanark is a Unesco World Heritage Site.

G Riverside Walks

Chatelherault Country Park consists of nearly 500 acres (200 hectares) of the Avon Gorge, one of the least polluted of the Clyde's tributaries. There are miles of riverside walks and picturesque sights here including the dramatic Duke's Bridge, the medieval mystery of Cadzow Castle, and rolling parkland featuring cattle whose lineage dates back to Roman times.

Above: the Chatelherault Country Park is packed with bucolic charm.

CRAIGNETHAN CASTLE

The A72 now follows the twists and turns of the Clyde as it runs through a valley of soft-fruit, tomato and vegetable growers, past Dalserf's 1655 church and the pretty half-timbered village of Rosebank with its three-star Popinjay Hotel (tel: 01555-860 441). Slightly further on, a sign points right to **Craignethan Castle** ⑤ (Apr–Sept Mon–Sun 9.30am–6.30pm, 1 Nov–31 Mar Sat 9.30am–5.30pm, Sun 2–4.30pm, last entry 4pm; charge), a sombre keep situated 2 miles (3km) up a narrow and twisting road. Dating back to around 1530, this rambling ruin was one of the last great family tower fortresses, and from it the Hamilton family played a pivotal role in Scottish politics, including supporting Mary, Queen of Scots, whom they sheltered here after her abdication in 1567.

Although Sir Walter Scott denied that its ivy-clad ruins were the inspiration for Tillietudlem Castle in the Waverley novel *Old Mortality* – and indeed he is said to have considered settling here instead of Abbotsford – its remote location and air of mystery are resonant for many of Claverhouse and the Covenanting bands.

LANARK AND NEW LANARK

Back on the A72, the road continues through Kirkfieldbank to the historic town of **Lanark**, a slope trodden during the Wars of Independence (1286–1328) by the raggle-taggle hordes of William Wallace, whose statue looks down from an 18th-century church along a bustling main street divided by pretty floral displays. This busy market town was founded in 1140 by King David, who established a castle here, which has long since disappeared.

Following the signs at the top of the street for New Lanark, the road twists down again to the Clyde and one of the most remarkable episodes in Scotland's industrial history, as well as one of its most adventurous heritage restoration projects. At first sight, **New Lanark** ❻ (tel: 01555-661 345; June–Aug daily 10.30am–5pm, Sept–May 11am–5pm; charge) seems little more than a group of stone-built warehouses, but it was here that David Dale and his son-in-law Robert Owen conducted a social experiment that was to have lasting repercussions for the bitterly oppressed working classes.

Dale, from Stewarton, made his fortune in weaving and French yarns and in 1785, using the abundant water power of the Clyde, set up the New Lanark Mills which, at their height, employed over 2,000 workers, many of them children. Along with Owen, who assumed management in 1799, he introduced a regime of decent housing, reasonable wages, education and health care, to prove his theory that contented workers were productive workers. His message did as much to create a social revolution as the mills had done for industry, and as a result workers' rights began to be considered seriously elsewhere.

The village, now a Unesco World Heritage Site, has been restored as a living community complete with hotel and shops, and the millworkers' tenement rows are desirable properties. There is also a youth hostel here (tel: 01555-666 710). In the Visitor Centre, a chair ride called the Millennium Experience compares in audiovisuals the life in the mill, past, present and future.

Along the river, a sylvan walk leads to the **Falls of Clyde**, where the Scottish Wildlife Trust organises badger watches, and the keen-eyed may spot kingfishers, owls and pipistrelle bats as night descends.

Below: the hunting lodge at Chatelherault Country Park was sensitively restored in the 1980s.

Travel Tips

Active Pursuits

For all its municipal grandeur and urban chic, this 'dear green place' is surrounded by hills and water and full of things to do.

Walkers are less than an hour away from the splendours of Loch Lomond and the Trossachs National Park (see feature p.108), which has Monros, Corbetts, heather hill rambles, forest walks and nature trails that will allow you to glimpse some of the 500 species of flowering plant and 250 species of bird that reside here. For the really serious outdoors enthusiast, there's the West Highland Way to explore, which takes about five to seven days to walk. It takes you from Milngavie, just north of Glasgow, to Fort William, a distance of 92 miles (148km), passing through some of Scotland's most stunning scenery. For information on all the walks that can be done in this area, visit www. lochlomond-trossachs.org.

BOATING

Glasgow is a city built on its maritime might, but it's only in recent years that marinas and boat clubs have really started to pop up. Sail out of the Firth of Clyde and head north along the shores and you will

Above: cycling along a canal towpath.

be gobsmacked by the beauty of the sea lochs, rocky outcrops and inlets, not to mention the isles of Islay and Mull. Experienced sailors should visit www.westcoastboating. org for information on all the routes, charts, sites, nature and companies that offer boats for hire. For those who can't sail but want to go out on the open wave, the *Waverley* (www.waverleyexcursions.co.uk) is the last seagoing paddle steamer in the world and does summer sails along the Clyde, as well as to the northern lochs and the nearby islands of Arran, Bute and Mull.

Previous Pages: natural splendours await for those keen to get active.
Left: the PS *Waverley* paddle steamer
Above: boating is popular.

CYCLING

There are lots of cycle paths around Glasgow and along the Clyde. Within the city, the Glasgow Mountain Bike Circuit in Pollok Park has a green circuit for those wanting a gentle ride through the woods; a blue circuit for a bit of bounce and climb, and a red circuit for those who want really rugged terrain. You can rent a bike from www.cosybike.co.uk.

FISHING

One benefit of the demise of heavy industry is that the Clyde is less polluted now, and trout and salmon have returned. Angling is becoming increasingly popular on the banks of the rivers of Glasgow. The United Clyde Angling Protective Association Ltd looks after the Clyde and its tributaries, and you can buy a permit from local tackle shops to fish on a particular stretch.

Ⓕ Football's Old Firm

Football fans will associate Glasgow with its two big teams, Celtic and Rangers. The rivalry between the Old Firm (as they are collectively known) is embedded in the history of the city and passions are as fiery as ever. Joint initiatives to confront its nastier side continue: those who manage to get a ticket for an Old Firm derby (not easy) will experience an unbelievable atmosphere (even if the football isn't up to much). Celtic Park, otherwise known as Parkhead (or Paradise), is in the East End (www.celticfc.co.uk), whilst Ibrox, the home of the Rangers, is in the Southside (www. rangers.co.uk). Both do stadium tours.

Above: Old Firm clashes are notorious for their intensity.

Above: playing a few holes at the Pollok Golf Club, with the impressive Pollok House in the background.

GOLF

The Glasgow area has dozens of golf courses in and around the city. Douglas Park (tel: 0141-942 0984; www. douglasparkgolfclub.co.uk) is an attractive 18-hole course north of the city near Milngavie. Lethamhill (tel: 0141-770 6220; junction 8 off the M8) is a municipal 18-hole course overlooking Hogganfield Loch.

HORSE RIDING

There are a few horse-riding centres around the outskirts of Glasgow. Easterton Stables in Milngavie (www. eastertonstables.co.uk) offers lessons, or, if you can already handle a horse, you can hack along the dips and dells of Mugdock Country Park in the Campsie Fells, surely one of the most picturesque ways to see the scenery.

ⓚ Children's Activities

Glasgow is a city with activities for all age ranges. At **Hampden Park** (tel: 0141-616 6139; www.scottish footballmuseum.org.uk; Mon–Sat 10am–5pm, Sun 11am–5pm), Scotland's national football stadium, kids and adults alike will enjoy the Scottish Football Hall of Fame, and have an opportunity to tour the stadium.

Kelburne Country Park, which is located near Largs (tel: 01475-568 685), boasts waterfalls, falconry displays, an assault course and 'The Secret Forest'.

The refurbished **Summerlee Heritage Trust** at Coatbridge (tel: 01236-638 460) offers kids the chance to ride on an old tram as part of Scotland's only electric-driven tramway. While out this way, the **Time Capsule** (www.thetimecapsule.info; tel: 01236-449 572, with swimming and ice-skating among volcanoes and cavemen, is worth a visit.

Above: a falconry demonstration at Kelburne Country Park.

Themed Holidays

Whether you have a day, a weekend or a week, Glasgow is full of opportunities to learn a new skill or to do something useful.

Artistic breaks

Glasgow School of Art (tel: 0141-353 4500; www.gsa.ac.uk) is the alma mater of many of Britain's edgiest artists, such as Roddy Buchanan, Nathan Coley and Christine Borland. During July the school runs a summer school allowing you to learn and work alongside resident lecturers and guest artists located in a number of the studios across the campus, including the famous painting studios in the Charles Rennie Mackintosh Building. They can also accommodate you cheaply within their student residences (en-suite accommodation at Margaret Macdonald House).

Bagpiping

If you dream of mastering the bagpipes, you can learn to pipe at **College of Piping** (tel: 0141-334-3587; www.college-of-piping.co.uk). They do day and week courses at hugely attractive prices at their centrally located school.

Buddhist retreats

If you feel the need for some inner peace, you have a good chance of finding calm at the **Kagyu Samye Ling** (tel: 013873 73232; www.samyeling.org), Europe's oldest Tibetan Buddhist monastery. They offer a range of retreats and courses for all levels, covering all aspects of the practice. It's a two-hour drive from Glasgow or an hour and a half by train.

Cooking classes

The **Cookery School** (tel: 0141-552 5239; www.thecookeryschool.org) at Peckham's in Glassford Street offers even the most hopeless cooks a chance to learn how to bring food together in a tasty and attractive way. Choose from a one-day course in Italian cookery (making minestrone and pesto amongst other classic dishes) and a five-day course of cooking, eating and drinking.

Nature

The National Trust for Scotland's **Thistle Camps** (www.nts.org.uk/ThistleCamps) recruit volunteers to repair upland and lowland footpaths, control rhododendron and erect fencing. You can even learn to restore bogs in the estates and properties of the NTS, which include Ben Lawers, Ben Lomond and Brodick Castle in Arran. A week's volunteering includes basic accommodation and food.

Above: learn to play the most Scottish instrument of all at the College of Piping.

Practical Information

GETTING THERE

By air

Glasgow has an excellent international airport to the west at Abbotsinch (tel: 0844-481 5555), which is served by flights from all main UK airports and has connections to Europe and North America. It has direct motorway links to the city centre, a journey of about 15 minutes. A taxi to the city centre costs around £20 from a rank outside the terminal building. Frequent Service 500 buses (Glasgow Flyer Airport Express), which cost £4.20 one way and £6.50 return, connect with Glasgow Central (15 mins) and Buchanan Bus Station (25 mins). The Paisley Gilmour Street Railway Station is closest to the airport; around eight trains an hour depart for the city centre.

British Airways and British Midland operate shuttle flights from London. British Airways (tel: 0870-850 9850;

Below: the Clyde Arc, also known as 'Squinty Bridge', was opened to vehicle traffic in 2007.

www.britishairways.com) operates flights from Heathrow. British Midland (tel: 0870-607 0555; www.flybmi. com) fly to and from Heathrow and Manchester. Easyjet (tel: 0870-600 0000; www.easyjet.com) also connect Glasgow with the southeastern airports Stansted, Luton and Gatwick, as well as Bristol, Belfast and the European hub of Paris Charles de Gaulle. Ryanair (tel: 0870-728 0280; www. ryanair.com) operates from Stansted to Prestwick, which is about 40 minutes south of Glasgow near Ayr – but has efficient road and rail links. There are also direct flights available to various other UK, European and North American destinations. For details of flights, and to book tickets online, visit www.glasgowairport.com and www. gpia.co.uk.

By car

From the south, the west-coast route follows the M1 to Birmingham, then the M6 to the Scottish border, then the A74 and M74, which joins the M8 into the city. The slower east-coast route follows the M1 and A1 into Edinburgh, then the cross-country M8 to Glasgow. From the north, the A9 joins the M9 near Stirling and then the M80, A80 and M8 into Glasgow.

By coach

National Express (tel: 0870-580 8080; www.nationalexpress.com) runs a regular coach service from all points in England and Wales into Buchanan Bus Station.

By rail

Virgin Railways (tel: 0845-722 2333; www.virgintrains.co.uk) operates the main west-coast route from London, Birmingham and Manchester; standby

Above: pedestrian walkways make it straightforward to get around on foot.

fares are cheaper but subject to availability. Queen Street Station has a shuttle to Edinburgh and serves the north. For general rail enquiries in Glasgow and Scotland: tel: 0845-755 0033; www.firstgroup.com/scotrail. Buy tickets online at www.thetrainline.com.

GETTING AROUND

On foot

A colour-coded sign system facilitates navigation of the city centre and main visitor areas. The distinctive blue panels provide directions and information about sights, maps and pedestrian routes. The Glasgow Tourist Information Centre on George Square *(see p.123)* has decent free maps and some more detailed ones for a few pounds.

By public transport

Glasgow's subway network is one of the oldest in the world, but 15 stations on a 24-minute circular track mean that no journey will take longer than 12 minutes. Packages are available, such as the Family Day Tripper Tickets (unlimited travel on First Scotrail services, subway, some ferries and many bus operators). A single ticket costs £1.20. The Subway's 'Discovery' ticket is good value: for £2.50 you can enjoy one day's unlimited travel after 9.30am Monday to Saturday and all day Sunday.

Above ground, First Scotrail (www.firstgroup.com/scotrail) runs the extensive rail network. Glasgow Central Station serves the South and England while Queen Street Station handles trains to and from Edinburgh and the north. City Sightseeing Glasgow runs open-air bus tours from George Square. National Express, Citylink and Megabus coach companies operate out of Buchanan Street Bus Station.

Car hire and parking

Glasgow city-centre traffic is heavy, but a car is useful for excursions to outlying areas. Car-hire firms in Glasgow include: **Arnold Clark** (tel: 0141-434 0480), **Avis** (tel: 0870-608 6339) and **Europcar** (tel: 0141-418 0040).

G Cycling

There are great cycle paths, including the 21-mile (34km) Glasgow to Loch Lomond Cycleway, from Bell's Bridge, beside the Clyde Auditorium on the Clyde, to Balloch. Bikes are carried free on all Strathclyde Passenger Transport-supported rail services. For information on cycle routes, visit www.sustrans.org.uk, tel: 0845-113 0065, or ask for the *Clyde and Loch Lomond Cycleway* leaflet at the tourist office.

Above: Glasgow and its surrounding area has many clear cycle paths.

Car parks are plentiful but busy, with spaces around St Enoch Square filled by mid-morning. Multistorey car parks are at Mitchell Street, Cambridge Street, Montrose Street, Waterloo Street, Oswald Street and Buchanan Galleries. Unauthorised parking is not advisable, as tow-away trucks and clamping units abound. If your accommodation is in the West End, take the subway into the city centre.

Steamer and seaplane

The world's last surviving paddle steamer, the PS *Waverley* (tel: 0845-130 4647), has a home berth at Pacific Quay by Glasgow Science Centre. A relic of the great days of steam, its massive engines are still open for inspection on summer cruises down the Firth of Clyde to Rothesay, Arran and the Kyles of Bute (www.waverley excursions.co.uk).

For a breathtaking flight to Loch Lomond, Tobermory, Oban and the west coast, charter a Loch Lomond Seaplane (tel: 0870-242 1457/01436-675 030; www.lochlomondseaplanes.com). Planes take off from a purpose-built dock by the Glasgow Science Centre.

Above: a vintage transport sign.

Taxis

Black taxis are licensed by Glasgow City Council and can be flagged down in the street, but there are also many private taxi firms which are slightly cheaper.

FACTS FOR THE VISITOR

Disabled travellers

The Glasgow Tourist Information centre dispenses advice and leaflets for disabled travellers and details about access. The city's main sights have improved provision and access in recent years. For information on disabled access regarding Glasgow's hotels and other businesses, consult www.disabledgo.info.

Emergencies

Fire, Police, Ambulance: tel: 999
Fire HQ: (north of the river) Port Dundas Road, tel: 0141-302 3333; (south of the river) McFarlane Street, tel: 0141-552 8222
Strathclyde Police HQ: 173 Pitt Street, tel: 0141-532 2000
Royal Infirmary: Castle Street, tel: 0141-211 4000
Western Infirmary: Dumbarton Road, tel: 0141-211 2000

Opening hours

Glasgow city-centre shops are gener-

Left: a Loch Lomond seaplane returns to land at its floating dock in Glasgow.

ally open 9am–5.30pm (Mon–Sat). Many stores stay open later – some until 8pm – on a Thursday. Sunday opening is now common in the city centre: noon–5pm is the norm.

Most major banks open 9.30am–4.30pm weekdays; some open Saturday mornings until 12.30pm.

Postal services

Most post offices are open Monday to Friday 9am to 5.30pm, and Saturday 9am to 12.30–1pm. For help and advice on all Post Office counter services, tel: 08457-223 344; www.postoffice.co.uk.

Tourist information

The **Glasgow Tourist Information Centre**, 11 George Square (tel: 0141-204 4400; www.seeglasgow.com; Mon–Sat May, June and Sept 9am–7pm, July–Aug 9am–8pm, Oct–Apr 9am–6pm, all year Sun 10am–6pm), provides practical guidance on getting around the city and the surrounding areas. Staff are on hand to help with information on tours and the city's historical and cultural attractions, as well as providing an ac-

Above: crowds at the busy Queen Street train station.

commodation booking service and a small shop.

Bureaux de change can be found at **American Express** (115 Hope Street, tel: 0870-600 1060/0141-204 0860) and **Thomas Cook** (15–17 Gordon Street, tel: 0845-308 9309).

F Gay and Lesbian Scene

Glasgow has a thriving gay scene and is home to Scotland's biggest gay festival, Glasgay (Sept–Nov), which encompasses everything from film to club nights. Glasgay's **Q! Gallery** (87–91 Saltmarket; tel: 0141-552 7578; www.qgallery.org; Mon–Fri 11am–5pm) showcases art and has a bookstore. Popular gay-lesbian hangouts are centred on the Merchant City and include **Delmonica's** (68 Virginia Street; tel: 0141-552 4803) – for food, cabaret and club nights – and **Revolver Bar** (11a John Street; tel: 0141-553-2456), a stylish place big

on home-cooked food and friendliness. For more information and latest listings check out www.glasgay.co.uk and www.gayscotland.com.

Above: girls' night out.

Accommodation

Glasgow's hotels range from the swanky and expensive to homely B&Bs housed in handsome Victorian houses. Some new boutique hotels – some contemporary-style new builds and others imaginative conversions of historic buildings – have been added in recent years, which have upped the standards generally. Look out for the new luxury hotel and spa, The Hamilton, currently being incorporated into the old BBC building and due to open in 2011. The Glasgow Tourist Information Centre (see p.123) provides an accommodation service.

Prices of hotels listed here vary seasonally; the ranges below (quoted as a guide only) suggest prices for one night in a double room on a bed-and-breakfast basis in peak season:

££££   over £150
£££   £100–150
££   £60–100
£   under £60

CENTRAL GLASGOW AND MERCHANT CITY

ABode Glasgow
129 Bath Street; tel: 0141-221 6789; www.abodehotels.co.uk.
Located in an elegant Edwardian Bath Street building which once housed the atmospheric Arthouse Hotel. New landlords ABode have added mainstream design touches and modern comforts, plus the fabulous Michael Caines restaurant and basement BarMC. £££

Cathedral House
28–32 Cathedral Square; tel: 0141-552 3519; www.cathedralhouse.com.
Atmospheric hotel set in red-sandstone Victorian Gothic mansion. As befits its proximity to the Necropolis, it's said to be haunted – ask about room 7. ££

Hotel du Vin at One Devonshire Gardens
1 Devonshire Gardens, Great Western Road; tel: 0141-339 2001; www.hotelduvin.com.
Luxurious accommodation in an elegant tree-lined terrace comprising five sandstone houses. Quality and comfort abound, from the Egyptian cotton bedding to the whisky Snug and its 'Glasgow Restaurant of the Year'-winning restaurant. ££££

Radisson SAS Hotel
301 Argyle Street; tel: 0141-204 3333; www.radissonsas.com.
Around the corner from Glasgow Central Station, the jaw-dropping glass-fronted lobby area impresses anyone interested in contemporary design. The cavernous art-filled atrium bar is a social hub while the Collage bar and restaurant has picked up awards. Standard modern rooms can seem a tad dull but the corner suites are gorgeous. £££

Above: a truly luxurious bathing experience at the Hotel du Vin at One Devonshire Gardens.

Above: the stylish bar at ABode Glasgow.

WEST END AND BY THE CLYDE

Alamo Guest House
46 Gray Street, Kelvingrove; tel: 0141-239 3395; www.alamoguesthouse.com.
A popular family-run hotel opposite Kelvingrove Park set in a grand terraced house. Their range of cosy guest rooms are simply furnished, well maintained and offer great value. £

City Inn
Finnieston Quay; tel: 0141-240 1002; www.cityinn.com/glasgow.
A stylish yet comfortable place to stay right next to the Clyde, with a fresh contemporary design and beguiling café-bar with views of the river from the terrace. Free Wi-fi in every room. ££

Crowne Plaza Glasgow
Congress Road; tel: 0141-306 9988; www.ichotelsgroup.com.
Modern high-rise by the Clyde, situated beside the SECC, offering a range of functional rooms and suites, a grand reception with bar-restaurant and shop, and a pool. £££

Kelvin Hotel
15 Buckingham Terrace; tel: 0141-339 7143; www.kelvinhotel.com.
Family-owned hotel in the West End within an impressive Victorian building. Guest rooms have high ceilings and free Wi-fi. Their Kelvin apartment sleeps four and is ideal for families. £

SOUTHSIDE

Glasgow Guest House
56 Dumbrek Road, near Pollok Park; tel: 0141-427 0129; www.glasgow-guest-house.co.uk.
This B&B offers homely accommodation and is handy for the parks detailed in Tour 8 (p.84) and the airport. £

Mar Hall
Earl of Mar Estate, Renfrew; tel: 0141-812 9999; www.marhall.com.
Stunning Gothic mansion located 10 minutes west of Glasgow airport in Renfrewshire. Comfy rooms and suites come in calming hues. The Aveda Spa offers treatments and gym. ££££

Number 10
10–12 Queen's Drive; tel: 0141-424 0160; www.tenqueensdrive.co.uk.
The long-established Dunkeld Hotel has been spruced up, re-jigging the layout to make many rooms more spacious. Expect warm hospitality and professional service. ££

Sherbrooke Castle Hotel
11 Sherbrooke Avenue, Pollokshields; tel: 0141-427 4227; www.sherbrooke.co.uk.

A Victorian mock-Gothic pile with baronial turrets near Pollok Park. Tartan carpets, period furnishings and antiques give public areas a cosy atmospheric feel, while guest rooms have modern bathrooms, warmth and free Wi-fi. ££

NORTH OF THE CITY
Cameron House Hotel
Loch Lomond; tel: 01389-755 565; www.devere.co.uk.

This five-star hotel is housed in a luxurious baronial-style mansion in a stunning Loch Lomond waterside setting. There are first-class spa and golf facilities, and you can even arrive by seaplane. ££££

Dakota Eurocentral
Eurocentral Junction of the A8/M8; tel: 01698-835 444; www.dakotaeurocentral.co.uk

A stylish yet cosy hotel with lots of contemporary design touches and useful high-tech facilities, including free Wi-fi. Their award-winning bar and grill serves Scots fish dishes and the sweetest oysters from Borough Market, London. ££

Red Deer Vintage Inn
1 Auchenkilns Park, Cumbernauld; tel: 01236-795 861; www.vintageinn.co.uk/thereddeercumbernauld/.

Great-value accommodation with functional, clean rooms and a pub-style restaurant. Popular with anglers who cast off at nearby Broadward Loch. The Vintage Inns chain also has a hotel at Balloch near Loch Lomond. ££

WEBSITES
For a comprehensive list of hotels in the city, see www.glasgowguide.co.uk/hotels.html.

Guesthouses/Bed & Breakfasts: www.information-britain.co.uk; www.scottishaccommodationindex.com; www.laterooms.com

Green: www.organicholidays.co.uk; www.ecofriendlytourist.com

Self-catering: For those staying for more than a few days, an apartment is a sensible option:
www.citybaseapartments.com;
www.glasgowloftapartment.co.uk;
www.city-apartments-glasgow.com;
www.max-hotels.co.uk;
www.dreamhouseapartments.com

Below: the pool at the Crowne Plaza Glasgow *(see p.125)*.

Index

Credits

Insight Great Breaks Glasgow
Written by: Ron Clark, Colin Hutchison
and Nick Bruno
Edited by: Sarah Sweeney
Picture Manager: Steven Lawrence
Art Director: Ian Spick
Maps: APA Publications
Publishing Manager: Rachel Fox
Series Editor: Carine Tracanelli

All pictures by Douglas Macgilvray/APA
except: Abode Hotels 125; akg-images/
annanphotographs.co.uk 38B; Alamy 33T,
98; Axiom 81T; Bruno Bord 59; Tom Brogan
11, 122T; Crawford Brown/Rex Features 40;
Cornell Univeristy Library 8T; Citizens Theatre
Ltd 34T; David Cruickshanks/APA 4BL, 5TL,
25B, 28T, 29B, 41, 45, 54T&B, 57T, 58B, 62,
64B, 69L&R, 80B, 103, 104T&B, 123T; Jean-
Pierre Dalbéra 88T, 94T, 96B; Elspeth Durkin
36B; Epic Scotland 46/47; Fotolia 117T;
fotoLibra 5TR&BL, 100T, 106/107, 107, 113;
Getty Images 66/67, 66T; Giant Productions
Ltd 31B; Glasgay! Festival 123B; Glasgow City
Marketing Bureau 43B, 111, 116T, 118T;
Glasgow Film Festival 10B; Stéphane Goldstein
55T&B; David Grinly 4BR; Paul Hart 105;
Hotel du Vin 124; Hunterian Museum and Art
Gallery, University of Glasgow 78B, 79T&B,
80T; iStockphoto.com 2/3, 4TR, 5CR, 18B,
19T&B, 20T, 21T, 22/23(all), 24T&B, 26, 27,
30B, 33B, 35B, 36/37, 38T&C, 51, 52B, 56R,
70T, 71B, 76, 86T, 87B, 101, 108/109(all),
110, 116B, 118B, 119, 121T, 122B; Ilpo
Koskinen 60; Leonardo 126; Library of
Congress 52T; John Lindie 17B, 82B, 84, 87T;
James Macdonald 5CL, 32B; Graeme Maclean
117B; Seth Mcanespie 44B; Raymond McCrae
86B; Jim McDougall 90T, 91; Alistair McMillan
112B; Photolibrary 12/13, 63T, 102, 112T;
Pictures Colour Library 38/39, 48, 114/115;
Sheep Purple 25T; Colin Reilly 14;
Stuart Reynolds/Rex Features 50; John
Robertson 44T; Paul Robertson 37B; Scottish

Viewpoint 34B, 99; Scottish Youth Theatre
47B; stevecadman on Flickr 46B, 49, 61; Nigel
Swales 106B; Stephen Thomas 89B; Topfoto
42B, 90B; Ville.fi 43T; Nesbit Wylie 63B.
Cover pictures by: (front) 4Corners Images
(T), APA (BL & BR); (back) iStockphoto.

CONTACTING THE EDITORS: As every
effort is made to provide accurate information
in this publication, we would appreciate it
if readers would call our attention to any
errors and omissions by contacting:
Apa Publications, PO Box 7910,
London SE1 1WE, England.
insight@apaguide.co.uk

Information has been obtained from sources
believed to be reliable, but its accuracy
and completeness, and the opinions based
thereon, are not guaranteed.

© 2010 APA Publications GmbH & Co.
Verlag KG Singapore Branch, Singapore.
First Edition 2010
Printed in Singapore by Insight Print Services
(Pte) Ltd

Worldwide distribution enquiries:
APA Publications GmbH & Co. Verlag KG
(Singapore Branch)
38 Joo Koon Road, Singapore 628990
apasin@signet.com.sg

Distributed in the UK and Ireland by:
GeoCenter International Ltd
Meridian House, Churchill Way West,
Basingstoke, Hampshire RG21 6YR
sales@geocenter.co.uk